Taking shape

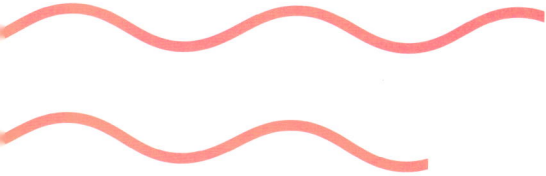

BILL LUCAS BRIAN KEANEY

Nelson

Thomas Nelson and Sons Ltd
Nelson House Mayfield Road
Walton-on-Thames Surrey
KT12 5PL UK

51 York Place
Edinburgh
EH1 3JD UK

Thomas Nelson (Hong Kong) Ltd
Toppan Building 10/F
22A Westlands Road
Quarry Bay Hong Kong

Thomas Nelson Australia
102 Dodds Street
South Melbourne
Victoria 3205 Australia

Nelson Canada
1120 Birchmount Road
Scarborough Ontario
M1K 5G4 Canada

© Bill Lucas and Brian Keaney 1991

First published by Thomas Nelson and Sons Ltd 1991

ISBN 0-17-433069-3

NPN 9 8 7 6 5 4 3 2 1

Printed in Hong Kong

Opportunities is an exciting new series of core books specially written to help you do well in your English lessons. *Taking Shape* is one of three books in the *Opportunities* series.

Opportunities will make sure that you are well prepared for the National Curriculum and for the Standard Assessment Tasks you will be taking when you are fourteen. It will not cover everything that you will need to learn. We assume that you will also be doing a variety of other work at school and at home. To be really good in English you need to keep coming back to things you have learned, to improve them.

We want you to be fully involved in this book, so we have made sure that it is very clear to use. You can use the Contents Page (on page vi), and at the start of each Unit there is a list of what you will have the opportunity to learn and practise.

At the end of every Unit you will find a list of the skills that you have been learning. You can discuss these with a friend or with your teacher; sometimes you may need to ask for more help.

Record sheets
At the end of every third Unit there is a Record Sheet. You will be given special copies of this to fill in. These will help you understand what you are doing and how much progress you are making. They will also help you to learn new words to describe what you are doing.

Your teacher will probably ask you to complete one at least every term. Once you have got to know how it works, you may want to fill one in more often.

Each sheet has a number of statements on it. You will recognise these from the ends of each Unit. Next to each one there are three targets for you to aim for. This is what they mean:

I understand this and have practised it.

I have done this with help.

I feel able to do this again.

If you are not sure what a statement means or whether you can do what it says, discuss it with your teacher.

These Record sheets will help you to know how you are getting on in your National Curriculum English. We suggest you should also keep examples of your best pieces of work and a record of what you have been reading.

Remember, you carry on learning English all your life. You will keep coming back to the same skills and improving them.

Finally, we hope you enjoy these books.

Opportunities has been written specifically to cater for the requirements of Key Stage 3 English in the National Curriculum.

We believe that the teaching of English – an international language with an extraordinary range of literature – is one of the most exciting activities for teachers in all phases of education. We hope this course reflects the excitement we feel for the subject.

Opportunities provides the core of what is required for Key Stage 3 of The National Curriculum.

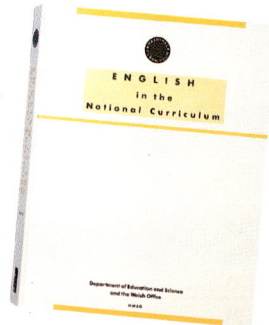

◆ It provides opportunities for students to experience the activities in the Programmes of Study for Key Stage 3 and so develop the skills essential for their success.

◆ It covers the range of knowledge, skills and understanding necessary for students to be able to tackle Levels 3 to 8 in the five Attainment Targets.

AT1 Speaking and Listening
AT2 Reading
AT3 Writing
AT4/5 Handwriting/Presentation

A series of three books such as these cannot hope to cover the complete range of activities, particularly in Attainment Target 2, which you will want to provide in your English lessons.

We assume that *Opportunities* will provide the core of the work you will want to tackle with your students.

Opportunities has been written with the model of English learning implied by the Programmes of Study in the National Curriculum firmly in mind.

We believe that this is essentially a model of English as it is really used. It follows that we have selected real language activities where the learner knows the context, audience and purpose of the tasks she or he is being asked

to attempt. The student is also given the opportunity for reflection within the different activities.

Allied to this we present language learning as a recursive activity. Young people, like adults, constantly learn more about how English can be spoken and written. They will therefore keep needing to come back to develop their competence in key areas. This is, of course reflected in the way that the Attainment Targets have been written.

There are three areas in which *Opportunities* is radically different from other English courses:

◆ It tackles knowledge about language.

◆ Students know what they are learning and assess how they are progressing.

◆ All three profile components – speaking, listening, reading, and writing – are presented as equally valuable and integrated naturally throughout the course. There are also more sustained pieces of language work in all books.

Opportunities is divided into three books to be used with the three years of Key Stage 3. The second book, *Taking Shape*, caters for Levels 4 to 7. It also reinforces work already covered at lower levels and provides opportunities for extension activities suitable for much higher levels.

The opportunities which this book presents are listed on the Contents page. Below are details of opportunities in Books 1 and 3.

Book 1, *Sharing Experiences*

◆ encouraging personal writing
◆ developing drafting skills
◆ studying sentences
◆ recording reading
◆ enjoying poetry
◆ unlocking the meaning of words
◆ studying verbs
◆ shaping and improving story writing
◆ understanding paragraphs
◆ looking at adjectives
◆ studying tenses
◆ looking at the subject of sentences

◆ setting out a script

◆ Operation Orpheus – a sustained project exploring environmental issues using role play, problem solving, work with environmental writing, charts, diagrams and maps, oral storytelling, play writing, letter writing, description work and reports.

Book 3, *Presenting Ideas*

◆ work with diaries and autobiography

◆ making a television programme

◆ looking at words closely, e.g. etymology, dialect

◆ recognising and using similes and metaphors

◆ the craft of narrative in prose and poetry

◆ literature, both classic (e.g. studying a scene from Shakespeare) and contemporary/ multicultural (including an interview with an Asian poet)

◆ writers and animals – work on fable and satire

◆ understanding the way words change, including paraphrasing and using synonyms

◆ developing an argument

◆ registers of formality

◆ bias and point of view

◆ keeping a talking log

◆ Operation Brainwash – an extended simulation in which the students are asked to solve the mystery of the disappearance of a young girl. This involves problem-solving, writing reports, prioritising, writing letters and devising a television advertisement.

Each book has nine Units. In the last three Units there is always a major sustained piece of work. It is not necessary to use Units in the order they appear, although you will find that some skills are developed in more complex ways in the later Units.

Clear signposting throughout the books makes them versatile enough to be used as an entire course or by individual students as a resource. At the start of each Unit there is a list of opportunities. These correspond to the Programmes of Study for Key Stage 3, but are written in a language that is accessible to students.

At the end of each Unit we have built in a moment of reflection and discussion for you and your students. The skills which have been practised are listed, again in simple but precise language. This time you will find that they correspond closely to the language of the Attainment Targets.

The model of drafting that we have followed is the one suggested by the National Writing Project and the National Curriculum Council. It encourages writers to understand the process of writing. Different writers will write in different ways. The drafting model we have adopted should be seen as a guide, not as a rigid formula.

At the end of every three Units we have included assessment materials to help students monitor their own progress. These profile sheets exist as a separate pack of photocopy masters and are provided in the free *Opportunities* Teacher's Resource Book.

The language on these sheets corresponds with the language used at the end of each Unit. We assume that individual teachers will establish their own patterns of use for these. You may wish to use these in conjunction with your own records when it comes to writing reports and completing Standard Assessment Tasks. We would suggest that students are encouraged to keep a file of their coursework/tasks.

We would also suggest that opportunities for student reflection, in addition to those which occur naturally throughout English lessons, should be provided at least once a term. In some cases it will be appropriate to use the profile sheets when a Unit has been completed. Once they are familiar with them, many students will wish to update their progress more regularly.

Throughout *Opportunities* all students will find something to enjoy and succeed at.

We hope to produce confident, articulate young people with a view of the world in which women and men are valued equally and in which all cultures are respected.

Bill Lucas

Brian Keaney

Contents

This Unit gives you the opportunity to

● *talk about a story*
● *find out how Standard English developed*
● *find out about dialect*
● *talk about your own language*
● *use speech marks*

This story is to be read aloud. A good idea is to get into small groups, and, as you read it, pay particular attention to how characters speak. You could organise your group so that you each read out what one particular character says.

The Firework Display

Norbert was hanging from this branch, swinging his legs about, and trying to break it off. If the Park Ranger came by and saw him, we'd have all been in trouble. Barry got hold of him round the ankles.

'Norbert, I'll do you if you don't come down.'

Norbert pulled his legs free, and moved along the branch towards the trunk. Barry chased after him and tried to pull him down again, but Norbert had managed to hoist himself up on to his tummy and was kicking Barry away.

'Gerroff!'

Barry punched him on the back of his leg.

'Well, get down then, or you'll get us all into trouble. Park Ranger said we could only take dead stuff.'

We were collecting for Bonfire Night. We were going to have the biggest bonfire in the district. It was already about twelve foot high, and it was only Saturday, so there were still two days to go. Three if you counted Monday itself.

We'd built the fire in Belgrave Street where the Council were knocking all the houses down. There was tons of waste ground, so there was no danger, and we'd found two old sofas and three armchairs to throw on the fire.

Norbert dropped from the branch and landed in some dog dirt. Barry and me laughed 'cos he got it on his hands. I told him it served him right for trying to break the branch.

'You're stupid, Norbert. You know the Park Ranger said we could only take the dead branches.'

Norbert was wiping his hands on the grass.

'I thought it *was* dead.'

I threw a stick at him.

'How could it be dead if it's still growing? You're crackers you are, Norbert.'

would you like it if I threw lumps of wood at you?'

'Don't be so soft Norbert, it was only a twig.'

Norbert picked up a big piece of wood, and chucked it at me. Luckily it missed by miles.

'You're mad, Norbert. You want to be put away. You're a blooming maniac.'

'You started it. You shouldn't have chucked that stick at me.'

He went back to wiping his hands on the grass.

'Was it heckers like a stick. It was a little twig, and it's no good wiping your hands on the grass, you'll never get rid of that pong.'

Suddenly, Norbert ran at me, waving his hands towards my face. I got away as fast as I could but he kept following.

'If you touch me with those smelly hands ... I'm warning you Norbert.'

I picked up a brick, and threatened him with it.

'I'm telling you Norbert ...'

Just then I heard a voice from behind me.

'Hey!'

It was the Park Ranger.

'You lads, stop acting the goat. You!'

He meant me.

'What do you think you're doing with that?'

'Nowt ...'

I dropped the brick on the ground.

' ... Just playing.'

'That's how accidents are caused. Now come on lads, you've got your bonfire wood. On your way now.'

I gave Norbert another look, just to let him know that I'd meant it. He sniffed his hands.

'They don't smell, anyway.'

Barry and me got hold of the bottom branches and started dragging the pile, and Barry told Norbert to follow on behind.

'Norbert, you pick up anything that falls off, and chuck it back on. Come on, Tony and Trevor'll be wondering where we are.'

The stick caught him on his shoulder. It was only a twig.

'Don't you throw lumps of wood at me! How

Trevor Hutchinson and Tony were back at Belgrave Street guarding the fire. You had to do that to stop other lads from nicking all the wood you've collected, or from setting fire to it. Not that it mattered, 'cos if they did we'd just nick somebody else's.

Mind you, I wouldn't have been bothered if our fire *had* gone up in smoke, 'cos it didn't look like my mum was going to let me go on Monday anyway. And even if she did, she certainly wouldn't let me have my own fireworks. I'd been on at her all morning about it while she'd been ironing.

'But why, Mum? All the other lads at school are having their own fireworks, all of 'em. Why can't I?'

Why was my mum so difficult? Why did she have to be so old fashioned?

'Go on, Mum ... '

She just carried on with her ironing.

'It washes well this shirt.'

It was that navy blue one my Auntie Doreen had given me for my birthday last February.

'I'd like to get you another one. I must ask your Auntie Doreen where she bought it.'

'Why can't I have my own fireworks, Mum? Why?'

She just wouldn't listen.

'I'm old enough aren't I?'

'Will you remind me there's a button missing off this shirt?'

'Aren't I?'

'I don't know what you do with the buttons off your shirts. You must eat them.'

She was driving me mad.

'Mum, are you going to let me have my own fireworks this year or not?'

She slammed the iron down.

'Oh, stop mithering will you? You're driving me mad.'

'Well are you or aren't you?'

She put the shirt on a pile, and pulled a sheet out of the washing basket.

'No! You'll come with me and your Auntie Doreen to the firework display at the Children's Hospital like you do every year, and if you don't stop mithering you won't even be doing that. Now give me a hand with this.'

She gave me one end of the sheet and we shook it.

'It's not fair. Tony's having his own fireworks this year, and he's three weeks younger than me, and Trevor Hutchinson's mum and dad have got him a £5 box.'

We folded the sheet twice to make it easier to iron.

'Then they've got more money than sense, that's all I can say.'

'I'll pay you back out of my spending money, honest.'

My mum gave me one of her looks.

'Oh yes? Like you did with your bike? One week you kept that up. I'm still waiting for the rest.'

That wasn't fair, it was ages ago.

'That's not fair, that was ages ago.'

I'd promised my mum that if she bought me a new bike – a drop handle-bar – I'd pay her some back every week out of my spending money. But she didn't give me enough. How could I pay her back?

'You don't give me enough spending money. I don't have enough to pay you back.'

'Why don't you save some? You don't have to spend it all do you?'

Bloomin' hummer! What's the point of calling it spending money, if you don't spend it?

'Mum, it's called *spending* money, isn't it? That means it's for *spending*. If it was meant for saving, people would call it *saving* money. You're only trying to get out of it.'

I was fed up. My mum was only trying to get out of getting me fireworks. She came over.

'Don't be so cheeky young man. Who do you think you're talking to?'

I thought for a minute she was going to clout me one.

'Well ... even if I had some money saved, you wouldn't let me buy fireworks, would you?'

She didn't say anything.

'Well would you ... Eh?'

She told me not to say 'Eh' 'cos it's rude. I don't think it's rude. It's just a word.

'Well, would you, Mum? If I had my own money, I bet you wouldn't let me buy fireworks with it.'

'Stop going on about it, for goodness sake. You're not having any fireworks and that's final.'

It blooming well wasn't final. I wanted my own fireworks this year and *that* was final. Blimey, kids much younger than me have their own fireworks. Why shouldn't I?

'Apart from being a waste of money they're dangerous.'

Dangerous. Honest, she's so old-fashioned, my mum.

'Mum, there are instructions on every firework. As long as you light the blue touch paper and retire, they're not dangerous.'

She started going on about how many people were taken to hospital every Bonfire Night, and how many children were injured, and how many limbs were lost, and if all fireworks were under supervised care like they are at the Children's Hospital, then there'd be far less accidents. She went on and on. I'd heard it all before.

'But I'll be careful Mum, I promise. Please let me have my own fireworks.'

That's when she clouted me.

'Are you going deaf or summat?'

'What?'

It was Norbert shouting from behind.

'Y' what Norbert?'

He picked up a branch that had fallen off, and threw it back on the pile.

'I've asked you twice. How many fireworks have you got? I've got over two pounds worth so far.'

Trust Norbert to start on about fireworks again. He knew I hadn't got any, 'cos we'd talked about it the day before. Barry didn't help either.

'I've got about two pounds worth an' all, and my dad says he might get me some more.'

It wasn't fair. I bet if I had a dad, I'd have plenty of fireworks. It wasn't fair.

'My mum hasn't got mine yet.'

Norbert snorted. He's always doing that.

'Huh, I bet she won't get you none neither. She didn't last year. She wouldn't even let you come.'

'That was last year, wasn't it? She's getting me some this year.'

If only she was.

'Well, she'd better be quick, they're selling cut. They've hardly got any left at Robinson's.'

Robinson's is the toy shop we all go to. Paul Robinson used to be in our class, but about two years back he was badly injured by a car. He doesn't go to our school any more. We see him sometimes in the holidays, but he doesn't seem to remember us.

'All right, all right, don't panic, she's getting them this morning, isn't she? She ordered them ages ago.'

I don't think Norbert believed me.

'Oh ... How many is she getting you?'

He isn't half a pest, Norbert. He goes on and on.

'I don't know. I'll see when I get home at dinner time.'

When we got back to Belgrave Street, Tony was throwing stones up in the air, seeing how high he could get them, and Trevor was riding round on my bike. There were stones and bits of glass all over the place.

'Hey, Trevor, gerroff! You'll puncture it.'

I took my bike off him, and leaned it against a rusty oil drum. Tony started to load the wood on to the fire.

'You've been ages. What took you so long? It's nearly dinner time.'

Barry pointed at Norbert, who was throwing a branch on to the bonfire.

'Ask him, monkey-features. We spent twenty minutes trying to drag him off a tree!'

The branch rolled back and nearly hit Norbert in the face. He had another go, but it fell down again. While he was doing this, Trevor crept up behind him. He grinned at Tony, Barry and me and took a jumping jack out of his pocket. He lit it, threw it down by Norbert's feet and ran over to us. Norbert threw the branch up again and this time it stayed on top, and just as he was turning round with a cheer, the jumping jack went off and scared the living daylights out of him. We all laughed like anything, but Norbert didn't think it was funny.

'Who did that? I bet it was you.'

He ran towards me.

Trevor pulled another jumping jack out of his pocket and waved it at Norbert. Norbert went for him, but Trevor was too quick. Norbert chased after him and got him in a stranglehold. Somehow, Trevor got out of it.

'Blooming heck, Norbert, your hands don't half pong. What've you been up to?'

Barry and me laughed our heads off. So did Tony when we told him. Trevor didn't. He ran off home to have a wash. It was dinner time by now, so we all decided to go home. Except Norbert. He never goes home on a Saturday. His mum just gives him some money for his dinner, and he stays out all day. I wouldn't like it if my mum did that. I went over to get my bike.

'See you, Norbert.'

Norbert had gone back to throwing branches on to the fire.

'Yeah. Mebbe see you later.'

'Yeah, mebbe.'

I started walking with Tony and Barry, pushing my bike, but then I decided to cycle on ahead.

'I'd better get going. My mum'll be getting fish and chips.'

We always have fish and chips on a Saturday. I pedalled off just as Barry called after me.

'We'll come round after, have a look at your fireworks.'

Oh blimey! I braked.

'Oh, I've just remembered, I've got to go to my Auntie Doreen's with my mum. My Auntie Doreen is doing her hair. I've just remembered.'

That wasn't a complete lie. My mum was going to my Auntie Doreen's to have her hair done, but I didn't have to go with her. Ooh, why had I opened my big mouth earlier on? They're bound to find out my mum hadn't bought me any fireworks, 'specially when I don't turn up for the bonfire on Monday. Why was I the only one not to have my own fireworks?

I took a short cut through the park. You're not supposed to cycle in the park but it was a lot quicker. Anyway, there was hardly anybody about and the Park Ranger was most likely having his dinner. As I was going past the swings and slides,

I saw this ginger-headed lad sitting on the kiddies' roundabout. It was going round very slowly, and he had a brown paper bag on his lap. Nobody else was about.

'Hey, you're not supposed to ride bikes in the park.'

He had a blooming cheek 'cos children over twelve aren't allowed on the swings and roundabouts, and this lad looked about fourteen.

'Well, you're not supposed to ride on the roundabouts if you're over twelve.'

He pushed himself round a bit faster with his foot.

'I know.'

He was a funny looking kid. I didn't know him, but I'd seen him around a few times. He was always on his own. I think he went to St. Matthew's. He held up the paper bag.

'Do you want to see summat?'

I wondered what he'd got in it.

'No, I'm late for my dinner.'

He stopped the roundabout with his foot.

'I've got some fireworks in this bag.'

I got off my bike, and wheeled it over. He did have fireworks in his bag. Tons of them. Bangers, volcanoes, silver cascades, dive-bombers, jumping jacks, flowerpots – everything. Every firework you'd ever seen.

'Where did you get them?'

He looked at me.

'From a shop. Do you want to buy 'em?'

'I haven't got any money.'

That's when I thought of it. I must've been mad. I *was* mad.

'I'll swop my bike for them.'

He got off the roundabout.

'All right.'

He held out the paper bag and I took it, and he took my bike and cycled off.

I must've been off my head. I ran home clutching my paper bag. I went in the back way, and hid my fireworks in the outhouse, behind the dustbin. I didn't enjoy my fish and chips at all. I kept thinking about my stupid swop. How could I have been so daft? I still had to go to the firework display at the Children's Hospital with my mum.

After dinner, my mum asked me if I wanted to go with her to my Auntie Doreen's.

'No, Mum, I said I might meet Tony and Barry.'

What I thought I'd do was go back to the park and try to find that lad and ask him to swop back. I mean, it wasn't a fair swop, was it?

'All right then love, but if you go anywhere on your bikes, be careful.'

I felt sick.

After my mum had gone, I went outside and got the bag of fireworks. I was looking at them in the front room when the door-bell rang. It couldn't have been my mum 'cos she's got a key, but I put the fireworks in a cupboard just in case and went to answer it. Norbert, Barry and Tony were standing there. Barry looked at the others, then looked at me with a kind of smile.

'We saw your mum going up Deardon Street. She said you were at home.'

I didn't say anything. I just looked at them. Norbert sniffed.

'Yeah. So we thought we'd come and look at your fireworks.'

Norbert grinned his stupid grin. I could've hit him – but I didn't have to.

'You don't believe I've got any fireworks, do you?'

Tony and Barry didn't say anything. Norbert did.

'No!'

'I'll show you.'

I took them into the front room, and got the bag of fireworks out of the cupboard. I put them on the carpet, and we all kneeled round to have a look. They were really impressed – 'specially Norbert.

'Blooming hummer, did your mum buy you all these?'

'Course. I told you.'

Norbert kept picking one up after the other.

'But there's everything. Look at these dive-bombers. And look at the size of these rockets!'

Tony picked up an electric storm.

'These are great. They go on for ages.'

The three of them kept going through all the fireworks. They just couldn't believe it. I felt really chuffed.

'I'd better put them away now.'

Norbert had taken out a sparkler.

'I've never seen sparklers as big as these. Let's light one.'

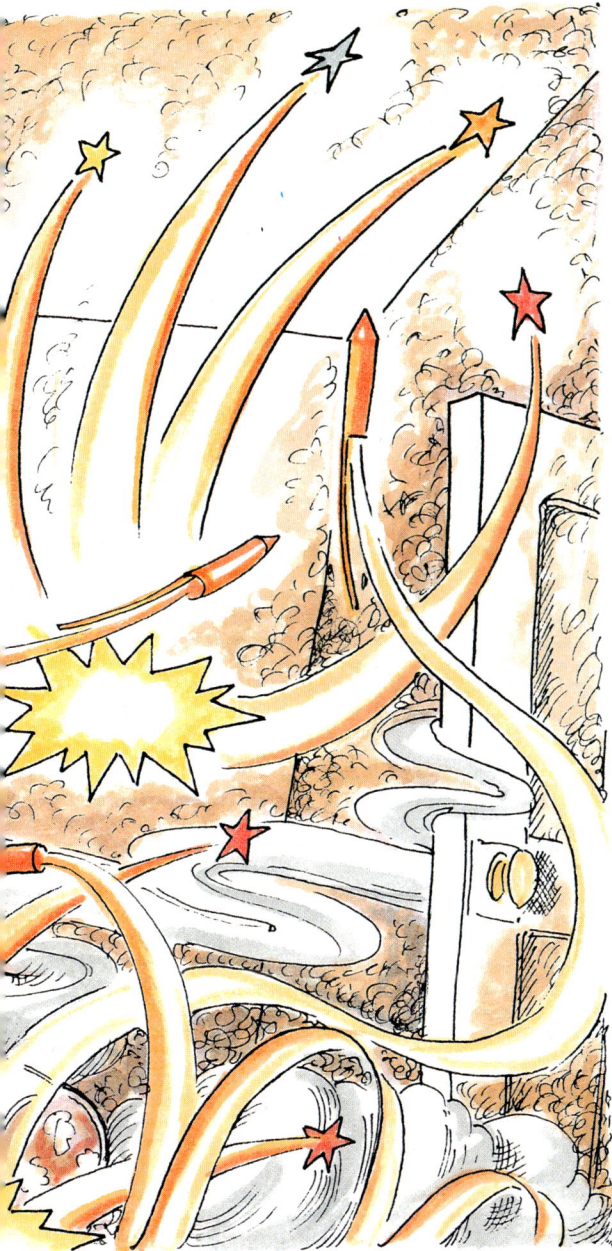

'No, I'm putting them away now.'

I wanted to get rid of Barry, Tony and Norbert, and see if I could find that lad in the park. I'd proved I'd got my own fireworks now. None of them could say that, now.

'Go on, light a sparkler, just one. They're quite safe.'

Well, what harm could it do? Just one sparkler. I got the matches from the mantelpiece, and Norbert held it while I lit it. When it got going, I took hold of it, and we all sat round in a circle and watched it sparkle away. Suddenly, Tony screamed.

I looked down and saw lots of bright colours. For a split second I couldn't move. I was paralysed.

Suddenly, fireworks were flying everywhere. Bangers went off, rockets were flying. Sparks were shooting up to the ceiling. It was terrifying. Norbert hid behind the sofa, and Tony stood by the door, while Barry and me tried to put out the fireworks by stamping on them. I could hear Tony shouting, asking if he should fetch my mum.

'Yeah, get her, get her, she's at my Auntie Doreen's, get her!'

I don't know how long it took us, it could have been half an hour, it could have been five minutes, but somehow Barry and me managed to put all the fireworks out. The room was full of smoke, and we were coughing and choking like anything, and I couldn't stop myself from shaking, and even though I was sweating, I felt really cold.

As the smoke cleared, I saw my mum standing by the door, her hair wringing wet, and all I remember thinking was, that I wouldn't need an excuse for not going to the bonfire on Monday.

George Layton

Using Speech Marks

You can tell what people say in a story because it appears in speech marks. These are speech marks. They look like this.

Although double speech marks " " are taught when you are learning about the different marks of punctuation, you will notice probably that published books usually use single speech marks ' '. Both ways are correct.

Using speech marks in a story is easy, because there are some simple rules to follow.

Speech Rule No. 1 – Always put what a character says in speech marks.

For example 'Are you going deaf or summat?'

Speech Rule No. 2 – Before you put the speech marks at the end of a piece of speech, you *must* use one of these:

a full stop   .

or a comma   ,

or a question mark   ?

or an exclamation mark   !

Speech Rule No.3 – Each time a new person starts speaking, you start a new line and a new paragraph.

For example

'Are you going deaf or summat?'

'What?'

There are other things to learn about how to set out the words you use before and after speech, but if you always stick to these three simple rules you will be able to write out speech clearly.

I In pairs or groups, look through the story carefully again. How many characters are there in it? Make a list of their names. (Don't forget George Layton himself.)

Decide which character said each of these things.

You're crackers you are, Norbert.

You're a blooming maniac.

Was it heckers like a stick.

You'll never get rid of that pong.

Stop acting the goat.

Nowt.

Oh, stop mithering will you?

Bloomin' hummer.

Are you going deaf or summat?

Y'what Norbert?

I've got two pounds worth an' all.

Huh, I bet she won't get you none either.

Hey, Trevor, gerroff!

We saw your mum going up Deardon Street.

Writing and talking are different types of language. What you say when you speak is often very different from what you write down. In your English lessons you will be finding out more about the reasons for these differences.

I In a group, look back at what the characters said in *The Firework Display*. Were there any words that you had not come across before?

Which words strike you as the kind of words that people would say but not normally use in their writing? (Make a list of them.) Why do you think this should be so?

One reason why talking is different from writing is that when we talk we do not always need to be so formal. For example, if you look at what the writer says to Norbert,

'You're crackers you are, Norbert.'

You can see that he could have said 'mad' or 'silly' instead of 'crackers' if he had wanted to. He also might have written 'You're' out in full as 'You are'.

2 In groups, look through the story again. In particular, look at and talk about what people say in it. Find some other examples of words which you would normally expect to be used when people are speaking one to another and write them down.

When you read the story, it is possible that you had not come across words like 'mithering', 'hummer' and 'heckers' unless you live in Yorkshire, where George Layton grew up. One of the most exciting things about the English language is the variety of words that you will find in different parts of this country and in different parts of the world. This is often particularly obvious when people are speaking.

3 In pairs or in groups, discuss what other books or stories you know that are set in Yorkshire.

How about films or television programmes that are set in Yorkshire?

Find out other words that are particularly used in Yorkshire. You might like to make a display of them with their meanings.

4 What do you think happened at the end of *The Firework Display*? What do you think the writer's mum would have said to him?

You could continue the story.

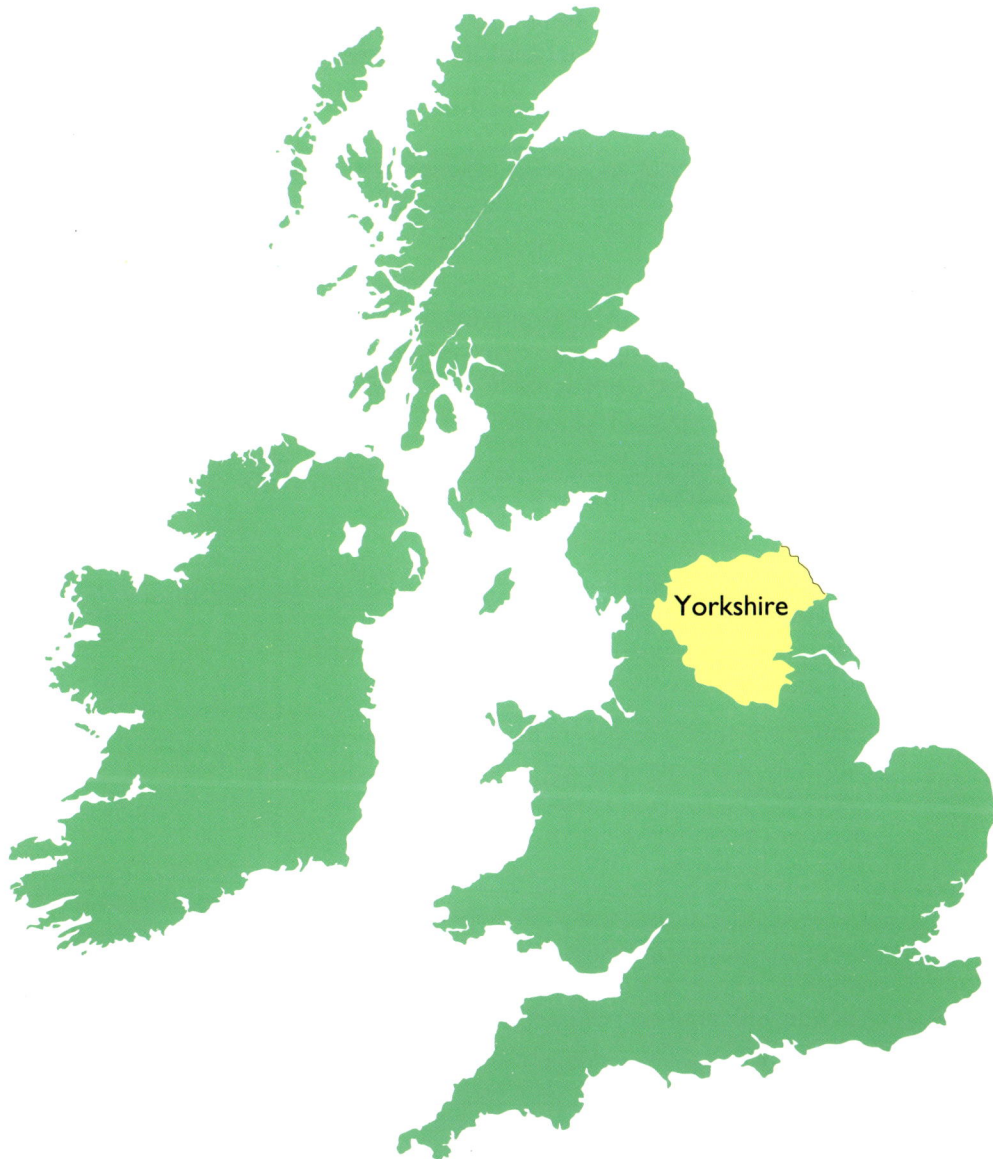

Yorkshire

You can't really understand how people have come to speak in different ways throughout the country unless you understand a bit about how English developed.

With this knowledge, it is possible to appreciate that what you have been reading and talking about is a **dialect** of English used in Yorkshire. A dialect is the distinct kind of language used in one particular region. Each dialect has its own special words, its own **accent**. (An accent is a way of pronouncing or saying words.)

When you know some of the history of the English language it will help to explain why someone from Northern Ireland sounds different from someone in Devon. It will help you understand why different words and sayings are used in Yorkshire and in Wales. It helps to account for the fact that in the area where *The Fib* is set they say 'brass' instead of 'money'.

1 In groups, talk about and decide how many different dialects or accents you know. Make a list of them.

2 How many famous people speak English with a strong accent? Find out where they come from. Using the map on page 11 to help you, draw your own map and mark as many accents as you know on it.

   Do you know anyone who speaks a dialect of English that you find it difficult to understand? Give an example of what you mean.

3 Are there any people you know who speak English with an accent from another country? Why might someone who was born in England still speak with this kind of accent?

   How many television programmes do you know which show people speaking in different accents? Add some of these to your map in another colour. Do television and radio affect people's accents?

4 How would you describe your own accent? Are there any words or sayings from where you live which you have found that other people outside your area do not understand? Make a list of them.

You could also make a list of any special words or sayings which you use in your own family or with your friends. Write them down, explain their meanings and share them with the other members of your group.

English Today

About 400 million people speak English today. Although more people than this speak Chinese, when you add in all those who speak English as a second language, this makes English the most widely spoken language in the world. After English and Chinese, these are the other most popular languages.

Spanish	español
Russian	РУССКИЙ
Hindi	हिन्दी
Arabic	عربي
Portuguese	português
Bengali	বাংলা
Malaysian	Bahasa Malay
Japanese	日本語
German	Deutsch
French	français
Punjabi	پنجابی

1 Which of these languages have you heard of? Which can you speak? For which ones do you know at least two different words and what they mean?

Try and find out in which countries all of these languages are spoken.

The world's different languages can be grouped together in families. Language families, like human families, are groups of languages which have things in common with each other. English belongs to the Indo-European family. This includes languages like French, Irish, German, Russian and many of the languages spoken in Asia.

A Changing Language

What we now know as English started to develop about fifteen hundred years ago. Since then there have been three clear periods during which it has changed considerably.

Old English 500–1100 A.D.

Middle English 1100–1500 A.D.

Modern English 1500 to the Present Day

Old English 500–1100 A.D.

The people who lived in the British Isles before this time were called Celts. They spoke their own languages. In the year 449 a number of tribes invaded the area we now know as England. They came from Northern Germany and were called the Saxons, the Jutes and the Angles. They conquered most of the southern part of England. Not surprisingly they brought with them other languages.

These new languages were all similar to each other and began to be called 'Englisc' or English. You may also find it described as Anglo-Saxon, a name made by combining the names of two of these tribes.

1 Although the Old English that you can see on page 13 looks like a foreign language, you would be able to recognise some words. See if you can guess the meanings of these words by using the drawings below as clues.

mete
sweostor
hus
mann
thusend
etan
drincan
sprecan

Middle English 1100–1500 A.D.

By about the year 1000, the southern part of Britain was called Angleland or Engleland and this was later shortened to the name we use now. For 500 years, while the Angles, Saxons and Jutes lived in England, the language called Old English was developing.

From what we know, it is likely that it would have sounded very different depending on where you lived. We also know that some words only existed in certain parts of the country. In Scotland, Wales, Ireland and Cornwall many people continued to speak the languages of the Celts.

In 1066 the country was invaded by the Normans who came from what we now call France. Their language was very different from what was being spoken in England. We do not know precisely what happened, but we can guess that Old English went on being spoken by many people in England, and that the Normans began to introduce their words and language. We know from the writers of this time that many French words were introduced. Celtic words also found their way into what was now called English.

During this period there was another invasion of a very different kind. In 1438 Johannes Gutenberg invented printing in Europe and from this time onwards books began to come into England. The first book to be printed in England was produced by William Caxton in 1485.

But in different parts of the British Isles there were already very different ways of speaking the language. This is not surprising if you consider that there had been four different invasions in the previous 600 years!

1 In your groups, look closely at the map.

Think back to what you have already found out about dialect from the story you read at the start of this unit.

Discuss the different ways in which someone speaks in Scotland, Yorkshire and London. What problems do you think this might have created for William Caxton when he tried to decide how to write down what people said?

Find out about the invention of printing. You could display your findings for the rest of the class.

Dialects and languages in the British Isles before printing arrived.

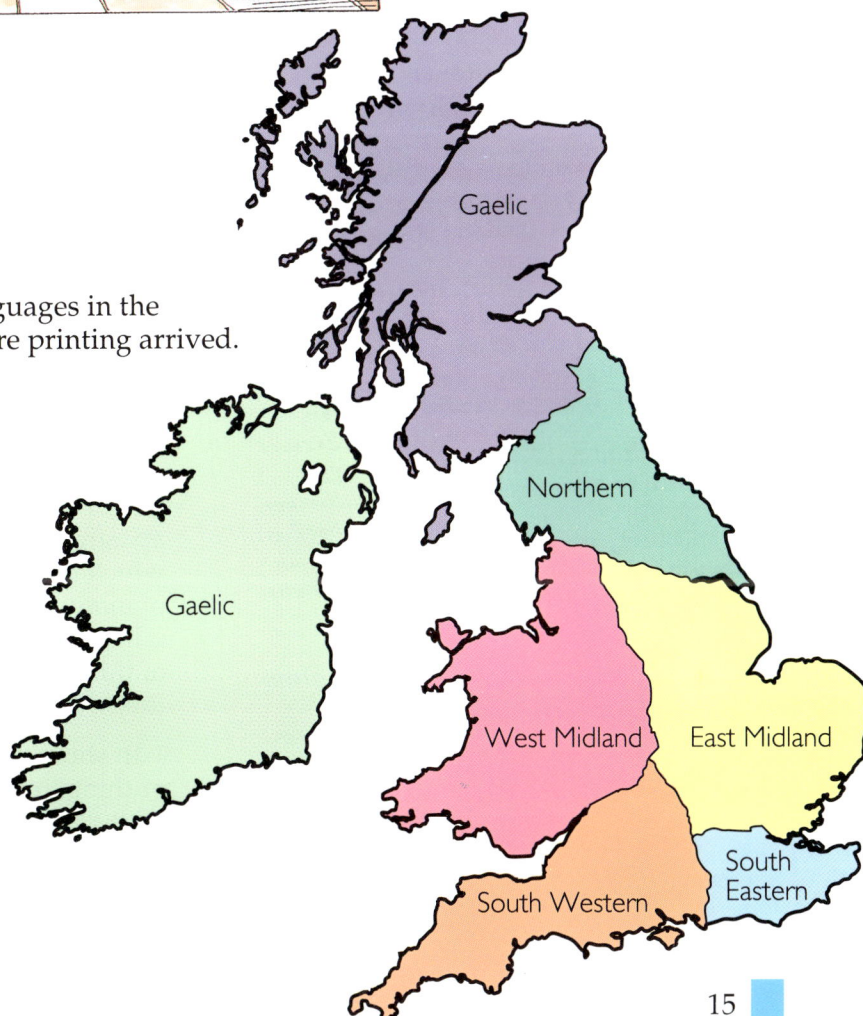

Modern English 1500 to the Present Day

The most important writer in the early part of this period was William Shakespeare. During this time the language continued to develop, with people travelling to all parts of the world and returning with new words such as potato, tomato and chocolate.

During this time something called **Standard English** developed. Standard English is the name given to the English that we can all understand.

When printing was first developed, the English that was most widely used by the printers was a mixture of the East Midland and London dialects. Standard English slowly developed from the dialect used in books. You can see this clearly if you look at the map on page 15. But Standard English is no longer just a local dialect. It is now used and understood all over the world and it can be spoken with many accents.

In some countries, like France and Spain, special committees of important people were set up to make rules about how the language of their country should be used. This did not happen in Britain, although some people have helped to change the way we use language. One of the most famous of these was Dr Johnson, who produced one of the first complete dictionaries of English.

In the last century, grammar books were used in all schools in Britain. These explained how the people who wrote them thought that Standard English should be used. In some cases they made up rules which they took from other languages to try and explain things. We still find rules helpful but it is important to realise that the English language is changing as the world changes.

The Invention of the Apostrophe

It is important to learn about how English works, and to do this it is helpful to know a little bit about its detailed history.

Study these two sentences. One of them is written in Old English.

Oswoldes boc

Oswold's book

What are the differences between the two? Can you understand both?

Originally many words ended in 'e'. Where something belonged to someone, as in the example above, the ending 'es' was used.

About four hundred years ago the apostrophe was invented to replace the 'e' which had begun to disappear from the ends of many words. Later it was used to show where other letters had been left out. Because of this we now use the apostrophe for the following two reasons.

1 To show that something belongs to a person or thing, for example, Oswold's book.

2 To show that one or more letters have been missed out, for example, from the story you have just read, 'I'll do you if you don't come down'.

DI'CTIONARY. *n. f.* [*dictionarium*, Latin.] A book containing the words of any language in alphabetical order, with explanations of their meaning; a lexicon; a vocabulary; a word-book.

Some have delivered the polity of spirits, and left an account that they stand in awe of charms, spells, and conjurations; that they are afraid of letters and characters, notes and dashes, which, set together, do signify nothing; and not only in the *dictionary* of man, but in the subtler vocabulary of Satan.
Brown's Vulgar Errours.

Is it such a horrible fault to translate simulacra images? I see what a good thing it is to have a good catholick *dictionary.*
Stillingfleet.

An army, or a parliament, is a collection of men; a *dictionary*, or nomenclature, is a collection of words.. *Watts.*

DID. [of *do;* bib, Saxon.]
1. The preterite of *do.*
Thou canst not say I *did* it.
What *did* that greatness in a woman's mind?
Shakespeare.
Ill lodg'd and weak to act what it design'd.'
Dryden.
2. The sign of the preter-imperfect tense, or perfect.
When *did* his pen on learning fix a brand,
Or rail at arts he *did* not understand?
Dryden.
3. It is sometimes used emphatically; as, I *did* really love him.
DIDA'CTICAL. } *adj.* [διδακτικος.] Preceptive; giving precepts:
DIDA'CTICK. } as a *didactick* poem is a poem that gives rules for some art; as the Georgicks.

I Look through the story again and find other examples of the apostrophe. Look through the last piece of written work you did. Can you use the apostrophe for these two different reasons?

Language is always changing. Some people have recently argued that the apostrophe should be left out. What do you think?

Speaking and Writing

It is important to remember that speaking and writing are different kinds of language. This can be very difficult. In this passage, another writer, this time from Lancashire, Bill Naughton, manages to bring his own dialect alive in a story called *One Small Boy*.

I Look at this description of an Irish boy called Michael who has moved to live in Lancashire. Michael is sitting next to a local boy called Charlie Criddle. They are both writing. Michael notices what Charlie is writing and tries to give him some advice.

In pairs, read it again, aloud if you can. Make sure you understand what is being said.

You might like to find some other stories or poems which have dialect in them. You could start to keep your own list of any words or sayings that you find with a note of where they come from.

Reflection

In this Unit you have been practising how to

- *talk about dialect and accent*
- *talk about Standard English*
- *talk about spoken English*
- *talk about characters and events in a story*
- *set out speech in a story*
- *write a story for an audience you have been given*
- *use the apostrophe*

Talk to your friends and your teacher about the things you have been doing in this Unit. Decide how much you have understood and how much progress you have made. Filling in Unit 1 of the Record Sheet on page 44 will also help you think about what you have done in this Unit and the knowledge you are gaining in your English lessons.

One Small Boy

He glanced sideways as he heard the rapid scratch of Charlie's pen beside him. He was able to make out the top line of Charlie's composition: *'When the manks cam they fun Heerward unconcon.'* He turned to Charlie.

'Stop!' he said. 'What's that?'

'What's what?'

'When the manks cam they fun Heerward unconcon.'

'What art talkin' about, McCloud? There are times when I think tha must be going off thy nut.'

'Read that top line of thine, Crid. Just read it.'

'I can see nowt wrong with it.'

'What's a *mank*?'

'Mank? Mank? Oh, tha means *monk!*'

'Then why not write monk, Chey?'

'Oh – flappin' Nora! Thanks, Mike.'

'Who's Heerward, Chey?'

'What the 'ell art talking about?'

'I said who's Heerward?'

'Heerward? Oh, Hereward – you piecan.'

'Then put *Hereward* – if it's Hereward the Wake. Chey, what's *fun*?'

'"Fun"? "Fun's" fun. I fun a penny in the street.'

'Tha'll fun four raps with her stick if tha doesn't change it. *Found*, you daft nut.'

'Oh holy mackerel, so it is, Mike. Quick, is there owt else?'

'Put an "e" on *came*. Chey, what's *unconcon*?'

'I'm blowed if I know what th'art talkin' about!'

'Tha'll be blowed if tha doesn't. Should it be "unconscious"?'

'Holy Moses, I were goin' at it that fast I didn't have time to cudgitate ...

Bill Naughton

This Unit gives you the opportunity to

● *develop your thinking skills*
● *read a story aloud*
● *explain and present ideas*
● *understand more about paragraphs*
● *argue a point of view*
● *respond to other people's ideas*

Speaking, listening, reading and writing effectively all involve thinking.

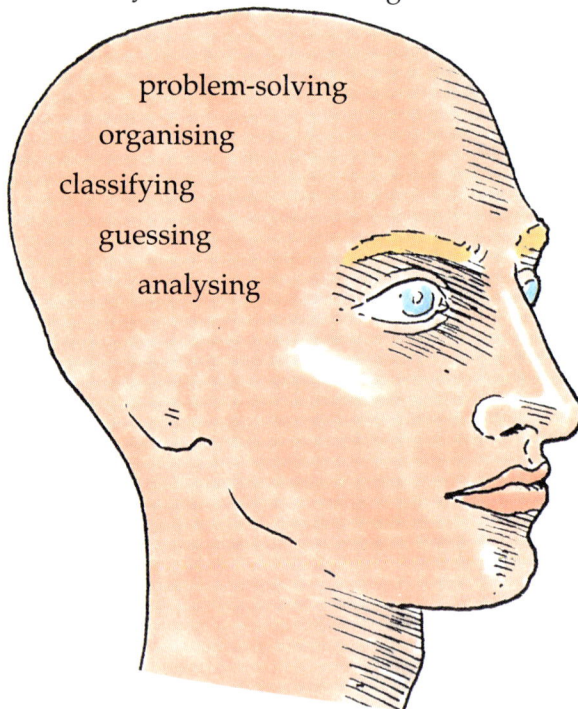

problem-solving

organising

classifying

guessing

analysing

Look up the meaning of any words that you do not understand. You will be using some of them later in this Unit.

In the next sixteen pages you will be practising some of the more common kinds of thinking to help you whenever you are using language.

1   In pairs, study this jumbled story carefully. It was originally written for a young child and is called *Cannonball Simp*. It tells how a dog is lost and then becomes the star of a circus. See if you can put it into the correct order. You can cut up the paragraphs on the repromasters in the *Teacher's Resource Book*.

The two pictures are included as clues to help you be sure you have found the first and last paragraph of the story. (The original order is printed on page 120.)

Cannonball Simp

A Simp became more and more worried as she talked to the other dogs.

'Who can tell what may happen now?' on said.

'You're not very pretty, are you? And you're fat and muddy,' said another.

'I doubt if anybody will want to give you home,' said a third.

B After the show, the ringmaster gave a party for Simp and the clown. He invited t little elephant, the lion and a monkey Simp had met, and they all ate until they were quite full up. The ringmaster told the clow and Simp that their act was the best the circus had ever had.

C And that is how she came to be called Cannonball Simp.

D One evening he took Simp outside the town and just dumped her near a rubbish p

E 'Got you,' said the dog-catcher. Two large hands grabbed Simp and she was put in the back of the van with the other strays which the dog-catcher had collected. Almost all the other dogs in the van had homes.

'We often get picked up,' they said. 'But what will become of you with no home to go to? And you don't even have a collar.'

F And so Simp lived happily with the clown and travelled round the countryside with the circus. The act became very famous and people came especially to see the little dog fired from a cannon.

G Then she came across the dustbins. She started looking through them for food and did not notice the cats who were angrily watching her.

H 'That's my dustbin,' hissed one of the cats as he pounced. Simp ran for her life with the cat just behind her. She was running so fast that she did not look where she was going.

I The van pulled into the yard of the dog pound. The doors were opened and the dogs driven towards the kennels. When the dog-catcher was looking the other way Simp saw her chance. She jumped up on some boxes and was away over the wall.

J Simp kept running until she was well out of the town. Then, because she was still frightened, she crept into some thick bushes to hide. By the time it was dark she had become very hungry and set off again down the road.

K The evening performance had begun. Just before the clown's act, Simp climbed into the cannon while no-one was looking. The man who was about to fire the cannon peered inside and, seeing Simp curled up, thought she was the ball. Simp's heart was beating fast as she waited for the exciting moment to arrive.

L Then, in the distance, Simp saw lights. They were the lights of a circus.

M Everybody seemed happy and friendly, but the clown was worried. People did not like his act anymore.

N She went towards them, hoping she might find someone there who would give her some food.

O The next morning the clown showed Simp round the circus. There were many tents, caravans and animals. Simp met a young elephant and a lion.

P Simp was what most people would call an ugly little dog. She was fat and small, and had only a stump for a tail. Her owner had found homes for her brothers and sisters but could not persuade anybody to take Simp. So, in order to get rid of her, he decided to leave her somewhere, hoping that somebody would find her and take her in.

Q Perhaps after that she could curl up under a caravan where it would be a little warmer.

R When it was light the next morning, Simp left the rubbish pit and wandered off in the direction of the town. She tried to make friends with people who were going to work, but nobody seemed to care about her. She spent a long time searching for something to eat but she could not find anything.

S She crept up to a caravan, climbed on a box and looked through the window. Inside was a clown who was very surprised to see a little dog peering at him. He opened the door and beckoned to Simp.

'You look very tired and hungry,' said the clown, and he gave Simp a large meal which she gobbled up. It was warm and comfortable in the caravan and the clown let Simp lie on his bed. She was soon fast asleep.

T The clown told Simp exactly what he did. He showed her the cannon which fired a rubber ball through a paper hoop. Just then the ringmaster came up.

'Unless you improve your act by tonight, you'll have to go,' he said to the clown.

U Poor little Simp watched the van disappearing into the distance. She could not understand why she had been left all alone. She did not know what to do. Then darkness fell. By the light of the moon she explored the rubbish pit and found an old armchair to spend the night in. Rats came out and looked curiously at her. When Simp said how hungry she was, one of them gave her a piece of bread.

'But you'll have to go in the morning,' he said. 'It's hard enough for us rats to live. There wouldn't be enough food for you as well.'

V Simp had an idea.

'That rubber ball is exactly the same size as me when I'm curled up,' she thought. 'I just have time to work out a plan before the show starts.'

W The crowds roared with delight when they saw that the 'cannon ball' was a little black dog. The clown was so surprised to see Simp that he almost dropped the hoop.

X The circus managers had a look of boredom on their faces as they watched the clown.

'He'll really have to go,' they said.

Y There was a roll of drums and WHOOSH! Through the air flew Simp, straight for the paper hoop. Right through the hoop she went.

Z Simp landed on a drum and stood there proudly while the audience cheered and cheered. She had really quite enjoyed being fired from the cannon. Then the clown and Simp were put on a horse and they went round and round the ring. Everybody was still wildly clapping and cheering.

John Burningham

2 In a group made up of two or three pairs, read out your version of the story, taking it in turns to read a paragraph aloud. Does it make sense? (You can check it by turning to page 120.) Do you think a story like this would appeal to a young child? Explain your reasons.

Which were the first two paragraphs you decided upon? Why? How did you do do this? How did you go about organising the other paragraphs in the story into the correct order?

Do you think this activity would have been different if you had been working with a newspaper report of a cricket match or a letter home from a nurse working abroad for a year? Explain your answer carefully.

All effective writing and speaking depends on organisation – giving the reader or listener information in an order that makes sense.

3 In a story, paragraphs are the main way that a writer can organise ideas.
Look at the story again. It is very clearly written because it is meant for children. Each paragraph has a main idea or subject and each one moves the story on. For example, in the first one we find out that Simp is an unwanted puppy, in the second the owner dumps her in a rubbish pit and in the third she finds out that she cannot stay there.
Go through about ten of the paragraphs in this story and complete this chart for each one.

Letter	Main idea / subject	How it moves the story on

In pairs, make up an animal story of your own suitable for younger readers or listeners. It might help you to visit a Primary or Junior school or a library and look at the books younger children read.

Starting Writing

Decide on the main events of your story and jot them down.

Composing

Write out or wordprocess your story in no more than 26 paragraphs and try it out on your partner.

Revising

Read it together. Decide on how you can improve your story. Make any necessary changes. You might like to think of new words or change the order in which things happen.

Proof-reading

Check your spelling and punctuation. Use a dictionary.

Publishing

Make a final and neat draft and read it to someone of the right age. You might like to illustrate it.

When you have finished your story, you could use a wordprocessor to copy, cut and paste it into a jumbled story, like the one you have been working on. Give it to someone else in your class to put into the right order.

To be a good thinker you need to be able to solve problems. There are problems all round you. If you open a newspaper or magazine you will see crossword puzzles and in some magazines there are quizzes.

Sometimes the problems are not just games. Many magazines print pages full of human problems which an expert will try to solve. You, yourself, may have had to work out how you are going to get from one place to another to meet up with your friends. In the next four pages there are some very different problems which all need solving.

What's in a Riddle?

1   In pairs, see if you can work out the answers to these riddles.

What wears shoes and runs for miles but does not have any feet?

What must you keep once you have given it away?

Little red man up in a tree
Stick in his hand, stone in his throat
If you tell me this riddle
I'll give you a groat.

A box without hinges, key or lid,
Yet golden treasure inside is hid.

A riddle is a way of describing something to get your interest.

2 How many other riddles do you know? Make a list of as many as you can. (Look out for some examples from other countries.) Try them out on other people in your class.

See if you can make up some of your own. You could make up your own riddles for a computer, a hurricane, a zebra-crossing, a hedgehog or anything else you can think of. You could try writing some in rhyme like two of those above. Try to make each one as puzzling as you can.

Some riddles can be longer and more complicated.

3 With your partner, study this riddle and the possible answer to it.

Romeo and Juliet are both lying dead on the floor. They are surrounded by water and broken glass. What has happened? How do you explain this?

One explanation is that Romeo is a cat and Juliet is a goldfish.

What other explanations can you think of?

The way to solve these kinds of riddle is to ask the person telling it to you lots of questions. This way you will gradually get to the truth. For example you could have asked:

Has the glass come from a window?

Did the water cause Romeo or Juliet's death in any way?

Is Juliet a woman?

What you say next will depend on whether the person telling you the riddle says 'yes' or 'no'. The trick is to think of the best questions to ask.

4 In your pairs, see if you can solve this riddle.

A man is found in a tree in the middle of the desert. He has hanged himself from a tree. The tree is perfectly smooth with no handholds below the branch from which he is hanging. He obviously could not have climbed up it and he could not have reached it from the ground.

A short distance from the tree a vehicle is parked. There is one set of footprints in the sand from the vehicle to the tree. These seem very similar in size to the shoes on the dead man's feet.

There are no other marks and there is nothing else in the vehicle that could have helped the man to reach the high branch. How did he do it? (The answer to this riddle is on page 120.)

This kind of riddle was made very popular by a man called Edward De Bono. He says they can be solved by a special kind of thought called lateral thinking.

Find out about De Bono. Find some other examples of riddles like this one. Make up some of your own.

If you like riddles, you might like to look at a chapter called 'Riddles in the Dark' in a book called The Hobbit *by J. R. R. Tolkien.*

In Unit 1, Language in the Making, you learned that there are many different dialects or local kinds of English in Britain. You also found out about different ways of speaking, called accents. There are also many different dialects of English throughout the world.

Back to Africa

Back to Africa Miss Matty?
Yuh no know wha yuh dah sey?
Yuh haffe come from some weh fus,
Before yuh go back deh?
　Me know sey dat yuh great great
　great Gramma was African,
　But Matty, doan yuh great great great
　Grampa was Englishman?
Den yuh great grandmada fada
By yuh fada side was Jew?
An yuh grampa by yuh mada side
Was Frenchie parley-vous!
　But de balance o'yuh family
　Yuh whole generation
　Oonoo all bawn dung a Bun grung
　Oonoo all is Jamaican!
Den is weh yuh gwine Miss Matty?
Oh, you view de countenance,
An between yuh an de Africans
Is great resemblance!
　Ascorden to dat, all dem blue-y'eye
　Wite American,
　Who fa great grampa was
　Englishman
　Mus go back a Englan!
Wat a debil of a bump-an-bore,
Rig-jig and palam-pam!
Ef de whole worl' start fe go back
Weh dem great grampa come from!
Ef a hard time yuh dah-run from
Teck yuh chance, but Matty, do
Sure o'weh yuh come from so yuh got
Someweh fe come-back to!
　Go a foreign, seek yuh fortune,
　But noh tell nobody sey
Yuh dah-go fe seek yuh homelan
For a right deh so yuh deh!
　　　　　　　　Louise Bennett

1 In small groups, read this poem written in a dialect from Jamaica. Don't worry about words that you do not know or do not understand and try to read it aloud fairly quickly without stopping. You could take a verse each.

2 Read the poem again at least one more time.

Without getting bogged down in the detail, what do you think the poem is about and who is Miss Matty? Use the title to help you.

3 What do you think these words mean? Which words in Standard English would you use instead of them?

Yuh haffe sey dat de fada bawn Mus

How were you able to decide this?

Some words are more difficult to work out, for example,

doan, Oonoo, dah-run.

What do you think they mean?

Some words are obviously special to this part of Jamaica, like

bump-an-bore, Rig-jig, palam-pam.

What do you think these mean? Does the fact that there is an exclamation mark at the end of the line give you any clues?

'Solving' a Poem

Some poems are a bit like puzzles, but with this difference – they do not only have one solution. To work out what they mean you have to 'ask them questions'. At the end of your questions you make up your own mind about what you think they mean.

1 Read this poem carefully several times on your own.

2 Make up a list of between five and ten questions that you could ask someone else in the class to help him or her understand the poem.

For example

What do you understand by the word 'specimen'?

Who do you think is speaking in the poem?

Get into pairs and try out your questions on your partner. Talk through your own different views of what has happened in the poem.

What do you think that David Kitchen is trying to say about the way human beings behave?

Join up with another pair and discuss this poem and what it means.

Specimen

And this is our rarest specimen of all
The last living human
Oh, you can see their bones in museums,
I know that,
But you will be one of the last of our
    community
To see one alive.
Yes, there were millions of them once
I've heard my grandfather speak of
Hunting them for sport.
A fine sport, too.
And fair;
Never more than six wolves to the hunt
So the human had a chance.
Cruel?
I don't think so.
They were hunters themselves, you know.
Our history says that
As the size of their weapons increased
The size of their brains got smaller.
No, personally, I don't believe that.
There's another theory that one of their
    weapons

Caused horrible changes.
Killed many of them and left their children
And their children's children different,
Helpless.
The history books find that too fanciful
But I wouldn't be too sure.
Oh, it has to be behind those bars
For its safety
And it certainly wouldn't survive
In the wild, anymore.
It's kindness really and,
Being a dumb human
It doesn't really understand its situation.
The eyes?
Oh, the eyes often water like that
It's part of the cleansing mechanism
For its vision.
Very effective, I believe,
But of no further significance.
Sad?
Well, yes I suppose it is
But that's progress isn't it?

David Kitchen

3 Make up and write out your own poem, suitable for a class display, about the last human being on earth, in which you present some of your own ideas about the ways we behave.

Starting Writing

Decide what kind of person your human is. List their qualities and use a spidergram to help you think about them. Decide if you are going to describe him or her and what you think about this human.

Composing

Do a rough draft in the form of a description (like *Specimen*).

Revising

Read it out to your partner. Listen to her or his comments and make any necessary changes.

Proof-reading

Check your spelling and punctuation. Use a dictionary.

Publishing

Do a final, improved and neat version of your poem. Illustrate it and add it to your class display.

There have probably been moments in your life when you did not have quite enough information to solve a problem and had to work out what was missing. Making guesses on the basis of the information that you have is an important thinking skill. You do it all the time when you choose a new book to read.

In groups, decide what you think has happened or is about to happen in the photographs on this page.

In your group set up some scenes of your own for which there is not sufficient information to be sure what has happened.

Stage 1

Decide on your situation, for example a wedding photograph, a party or a sport. Decide how much information you want to give those who are going to guess the situation.

Stage 2

Decide on one person to 'direct' your situation.

Stage 3

Freeze your situation at the moment you wish to show. In drama, freezing is a way of stopping the action as if it was a photograph or a series of statues. The person directing your group will need to stand back and look at the overall 'picture'. You may want to use one or two simple **props**. 'Prop' is short for 'property' and is the word used to describe any object used when acting.

Stage 4

Try out your frozen moment on the rest of the class and see if they can guess what is going on.

Stage 5

If you have a camera you might like to take your own mystery photograph.

A Grave Mystery

Archaeologists often have to make intelligent guesses about their evidence. As with the other ways of thinking that you have been developing, it is important to try and ask the right questions.

1 Look at this tombstone and the extract from the Parish Burials Register of that time.

Imagine that you are trying to find out where your ancestors were buried. You think that you have found one of their tombs but you are not sure. The writing on the tombstone is unfortunately very difficult to read and in places has worn away.

You have managed to find the relevant page from the Parish Burials Register, but it has a large ink-blot covering some of the information. It is all you have to go on to work out whose tombstone it is.

Use these questions to help you to start working out the answer and then make up some of your own:

Why is it clear that the tomb belonged to a man?

Using the Burials Register, which of the names can you rule out because of the date of death?

Using the writing that you can decipher on the tombstone, which of the surnames in the Burials Register do not seem to match the surname on the tomb?

The correct answer is on page 120.

R..... .....SON

b--rr Feb 1 1/96

died Apr 14 1841

Aged

also

MARY his wife

Burials Register

Rose Brown	Age 2	February 11th
Richard Barson	Age 15	April 12th
Roger Dawson	Age 18	
Robert Dawson	Age 45	
Henry Brown	Age	
Robert Carson	Age	
Elizabeth Dawson	Age	April 23rd
Roland Barson	Age 18	May 14th

Make up your own puzzle like this using a tombstone and one other piece of evidence.

Another important part of thinking is **classifying.** Classifying means putting into divisions, types or groups. You do it most of the time and may not even realise you are doing it. It is one of the skills that helps you to make sense of the world as you see it.

1 Look at and read carefully these two pages describing a typical Saturday morning on television.

28 April SATURDAY

BBC 1

6.40-7.30am
Open University
6.40 Maths: Coping with Irrationality
7.05 Data Modelling – the Wood from the Trees

7.30am
Playdays
The Playbus stops today at the Patch Stop where Peggy bird-watches and spots oily guillemots.
Patch's friend
................Vanessa Amberleigh
Storyteller: Simon Davies.
Producer Anne Gobey (R)

7.50am
The Muppet Babies
The babies are caught by the Hollywood bug and make their own video.
*Created for television
by Jim Henson (R)*.

8.15am
The 8.15 from Manchester
The boys are back in town! Charlotte Hindle joins New Kids on the Block – Danny, Donny, Joe, Jon and Jordan – on their first UK tour. Back in the station, Ross King opens a kissing gate and finds singer Sam Brown.
Also on the show: television's whizziest quiz, *It's Tough at the Top*, the continuing saga of *Defenders of the Earth* and two brand-new features – *Rapattack* and *Photoromance*.
Studio director Alan Yardley
Series producer Martyn Day
BBC North
(New Kids on the Block are guests on 'Wogan' on Monday at 7.00pm)

10.55am FILM
The Flight of Dragons
An animated adventure film featuring the voices of John Ritter, James Earl Jones, Harry Morgan, Victor Buono and James Gregory. It is a time between the waning Age of Magic and the dawning Age of Science: a century when wizards rule the earth and dragons rule the skies. It is also an era when one man is brought back from the 20th century to help recapture the Red Crown that empowers the evil Ommadon.
Producers/Directors
Arthur Rankin Jr and Jules Bass
● FILMS: pages 16-21

12.27pm Weather
With Michael Fish

12.30-5.05pm
GRANDSTAND
Introduced by Desmond Lynam from Wembley.
Provisional Timetable
12.35 Football; **1.00** News
1.05 Snooker; **2.00** Squash
2.25 Boxing; **2.40** Rugby
4.40 Final Score

Rugby League
From Wembley.
Silk Cut Challenge Cup Final. Wigan *v* Warrington. Live coverage of the match, with Warrington given little chance in the 'year of the underdog'. Commentators: Ray French, Alex Murphy and Martin Offiah.

Snooker
From the Crucible, Sheffield. Embassy World Professional Snooker Championship. The final begins.
Commentators: Ted Lowe Jack Karnehm and Clive Everton.

Football
1990 World Cup.
Group B – Argentina, USSR, Romania and Cameroon.
Reporter: Gerald Sinstadt.

Squash
From Wembley.
Hi-Tech British Open Women's Championship. Martine le Moignan defends. Commentators: Tony Gubba and Jonah Barrington.

Boxing
From Latchmere Leisure Centre. Gary Jacobs v Alain Cuvillier. Commentator: Harry Carpenter.
*Television presentation:
Rugby league Keith Phillips
Snooker Keith Mackenzie
Squash Campbell Ferguson
Boxing Bob Duncan
Producer Martin Hopkins
Editor John Philips*

5.05pm News
With Moira Stuart.
Weather

5.15pm Regional News and Sport

5.20pm
Stay Tooned!
Tony Robinson brings you more animated anarchy. This week he concentrates on musical 'toons'.
*Videotape editor Roy Demery
Producer Nick Jones*

5.45-6.35pm
The Flying Doctors
An Australian drama series. An explosion at a gas field injures Geoff, and Kate accompanies him for therapy at Broken Hill. Will romance blossom?
*Dr Geoff Standish
........................Robert Grubb
Dr Chris Randall......Liz Burch
Kate Wellings.....Lenore Smith*
● CEEFAX SUBTITLES

BBC 2

6.50am-2.45pm
Open University
6.50 Maths: Area Games
7.15 Health Visiting and the Family
7.40 Geology: Rock Textures
8.05 The Internal Combustion Engine
8.30 Technology: More than Meets the Eye
8.55 Information Technology: For You
9.20 Education: Literacy in Jamaica
9.45 Romantic Poets in the Alps
10.10 Measuring with Light
10.35 Religion: Pilgrimage
11.00 The Oldham Experience
11.25 Evolution of Fishes
11.50 Business to Business
12.15 Whose Countryside Tomorrow?
12.40 Statistics: Lines, Before and After
1.05 Open Business School: Mastering Management
1.30 Modern Art: Kirchner
1.55 Culture and Belief in Europe
2.20 Images of the Third World

2.45pm
Mahabharat
A 91-part epic drama. 3: King Shantanu falls in love with Satyavati and asks for her hand. But her father imposes a condition.
*King Shantanu
........................Rishabh Shukla
Dev Vrat........ Mukesh Khanna
Satyavati........ Debashree Roy
(In Hindi with English subtitles. Repeated tomorrow 11.45pm BBC1)*

3.25pm FILM
Battleship Potemkin
Starring **A Antonov Grigori Alexandrov**
Regarded as a milestone in world cinema, this was Sergei Eisenstein's second film. Intolerable conditions on the battleship *Potemkin* lead to mutiny, supported by the citizens of Odessa.
*Vakulinchuk.......... A Antonov
Giliarovski.... Grigori Alexandrov
Meisel score orchestrated and conducted by Arthur Kleiner
(In colour and black and white)*
● FILMS: pages 16-21

4.30-8.30pm
Live from Leningrad: Boris Godunov
A unique collaboration brings Andrei Tarkovsky's acclaimed Royal Opera House production of Musorgsky's masterpiece to the stage of Leningrad's Kirov Theatre where the work premiered in 1874. Tarkovsky left the Soviet Union in 1983 and died four years later. *Boris Godunov* was the great film director's only opera production. Tonight's conductor is Kirov music director Valery Gergiev. British bass Robert Lloyd makes his Russian debut playing the tormented tsar, Boris Godunov. The production is staged by director Stephen Lawless with designs by Nicholas Dvigoubsky.
*Marina
..........Olga Borodina (soprano)
Dmitry
...........Alexei Stelianko (tenor)
Rangoni
...........Sergei Leiferkus (bass)
Pimen
........Alexander Morosov (bass)
Varlaam.
.... Vladimir Ognovenko (bass)
Television lighting Alan Woolford
Television sound Graham Haines
Producers Peter Maniura and Dennis Marks
Director Humphrey Burton*
● SIMULTANEOUS BROADCAST: with Radio 3.

After murdering the rightful heir to the Russian throne, Boris Godunov (Robert Lloyd) has himself crowned tsar
Boris Godunov, 4.30pm BBC2

AT A GLANCE

BBC1

6.40	*Open University*
7.30	*Playdays*
7.50	*The Muppet Babies*
8.15	*The 8.15 from Manchester*
10.55	*Film: The Flight of Dragons*
12.30	*Grandstand*
5.05	*News and Weather*
5.20	*Stay Tooned!*
5.45	*The Flying Doctors* ★
6.35	*Opportunity Knocks*
7.25	*Three Up, Two Down* ★
7.50	*Film: Perry Mason: The Case of the Shooting Star* ★
9.30	*News and Sport*
9.50	*Casualty* ★
10.40	*Paramount City*
11.20	*Film: The Man with the Deadly Lens*
1.15	*Weather*
1.20	*Close*

BBC2

6.50	*Open University*
2.45	*Mahabharat*
3.25	*Film: Battleship Potemkin*
4.30	*Live from Leningrad: Boris Godunov*
8.30	*World Snooker*
9.50	*Video Diaries* ★
10.30	*NewsView*
11.15	*World Snooker*
12.05	*Close*

★ = CEEFAX SUBTITLES

Notes

■ The BBC does not broadcast before 9.00pm programmes that it believes to be unsuitable for children. After that time parents can be expected to share responsibility for what children see. Some programmes after 9.00pm may be appropriate for an adult audience only.

■ BBCtv programmes are in colour and shown for the first time unless otherwise stated.

■ (R) denotes repeat.

■ Feature films (except those made by the BBC) may have been shown before on broadcast service unless indicated as 'First showing on network television'; this does not take account of previous screenings on pay, subscription or satellite services for which a charge is made.

28 APRIL - 4 MAY 1990

In groups, decide what are the main groups or classifications that the TV guide uses to divide up programmes.

28 April SATURDAY

ITV
LWT

5.00am
ITN Morning News

TV-am

6.00 to 9.25am
6.00 News
Read by Susie Grant.

Good Morning Moments
Presented by Ulrika Jonsson.

7.00 News
Read by Susie Grant.

WAC 90
Michaela Strachan and Mike Brosnan with the Wac Wac game, Club Call, Ghosts, Monsters and Legends, and Singing in the Shower, plus at 8.15 Denver, the Last Dinosaur and at 8.40 Flop Goes the Joker, second of a two-part adventure with Batman. Write to: WAC 90, PO Box 21, Manchester M60 9GR.
PRODUCER/DIRECTOR
NICK WILSON
A Clear Idea Television Production for TV-am

9.25am
Ghost Train
FRANCES DODGE
GERARD
PAUL J MEDFORD
NOBBY THE SHEEP
SABRA WILLIAMS
with
MICHELLE COLLINS
CHRIS PACKHAM
THE VICIOUS BOYS
GHOST BOAT
Sabra and Paul think they are going on a Caribbean Cruise.
OZ
Jason Donovan shares breakfast with Gerard and Nobby.
POP
A sneak behind-the-scenes of one of New Kids On The Block's first UK gigs.
WAKE UP
Angelo and Andy go sailing.
SKULL
Will the Mafiettes be defeated this week?
CARTOONS
The Real Ghostbusters in The Devil in the Deep. Plus, Bugs Bunny.
TALES FROM THE CRYPT
Michelle Collins, Cindy in Eastenders, is roped into the crazy story game.

Ulrika Jonsson has something to smile about this morning, recalling some TV-am moments

COMPETITIONS
Jason Donovan is giving away his tent.

ASSOCIATE PRODUCER
ANGELO ABELA
SERIES PRODUCER
VIV ELLIS
PRODUCER/DIRECTOR
HUGH DAVIES

Anglia Television Production

ITV variations
Viewers in the LWT region who can receive alternative pro grammes from adjoining ITV areas will find that transmissions alter as follows:
TVS 12.30pm to 1.00 Rallycross; 3.05 to 4.45 Film: Escape of the Amethyst. Real-life story of frigate HMS Amethyst, starring Richard Todd and William Hartnell; 10.40 Film: The Stud. Joan Collins stars as a man-eater; 12.25am Friday the 13th; 1.25 The Munsters Today; 1.55 Raw Power; 2.55 The Twilight Zone; 3.20 to 4.05am Wrestling.
ANGLIA 3.05pm to 4.45 Film: The 1,000 Plane Raid. WW2 bomber drama; 10.40 Film: The Stone Killer. Charles Bronson as ruthless LA detective; 12.25am Film: The Valdez Horses. Charles Bronson in ranching drama set in New Mexico; 2.15 The Hit Man and Her; 4.00 to 5.05am In the Heat of the Night.
CENTRAL 12.30pm to 1.00 Water Sports; 3.05 to 4.45 Film: The 1,000 Plane Raid (As Anglia); 10.40 Film: The Stone Killer (As Anglia); 12.30am Garrison's Gorillas; 1.30 CinemAttractions; 2.00 Police Precinct; 3.00 America's Top 10; 3.35 Crazy About the Movies; 4.05 to 5.05am American College Football.

11.30am
The ITV Chart Show
The all-video chart show. The specialist chart is Rock. Vintage Videos features The Carpenters.
Digital Stereo Sound
SERIES PRODUCER
PHILIP DAVEY
EXECUTIVE PRODUCER
KEITH MACMILLAN
A Video Visuals Production

12.30pm
Huckleberry Finn and His Friends
LOVE IN BLOOM
Tom turns a punishment to his advantage.
Huckleberry   Ian Tracey
Tom   Sammy Snyders

1.00pm
ITN News
Oracle ITN News Headlines throughout the week, page 101 followed by
ITV National Weather

1.05 to 1.10pm
LWT News
and Weather
ANNA MARIA ASHE

4

6.00 to 9.25am
Early Morning
6.00 Comic Book
Cartoons for younger viewers including: Batman, Sleeping Beauty and Kaboodle.
7.30 International Times – World News
The stories behind the headlines.
ITN Production
8.00
Trans World Sport
International sporting news and interviews.
TWI Production
9.00 Channel 4 Racing: The Morning Line
Previewing the day's racing action.

9.25am
Sing & Swing
Performances by the stars of the Thirties and the Forties.

9.30am
Listening Eye
SIGN OF OUR TIMES
MARK DENMARK
RACHELL BASTIKAR
1: A Deaf Family
Six documentary films and two discussion programmes in which deaf people reveal their feelings about what it's like to be deaf in 20th-century Britain. 'It's great to have a big family of deaf people', says 15-year-old Tyron Woolfe. His enthusiasm expresses the positive feelings of children brought up in a household where everyone uses sign language. Tyron and his brother Ramon are the fourth generation to enjoy this privilege. Presented in British

sign language and subtitles. This programme was first shown last Monday. ‡

10.00am
Indian Screen: Vasantha Kokila
FILM Continuing this season of popular Indian films. Lakshmi is a beautiful young girl in modern India. Her budding relationship with the handsome Seenu is cut short when she is badly injured in a car accident and regresses to a child-like state. Seenu gradually helps nurse Lakshmi back to health. But will she remember him when she recovers? An Indian film with Telegu dialogue and English subtitles.
See film guide, beginning page 19
Seenu   Kamala Hassan
Lakshmi   Sridevi
Mrs Viswanathan
                Silk Smitha
DIRECTOR BALU MEHENDRA

12.40 to 12.50pm
The Clydeside Classic
Two of the world's top snooker players battle it out in the final of this special alternative tournament celebrating Glasgow as Cultural Capital of Europe.
PRODUCERS ANNA RIDLEY, JANE RIGBY
Fields and Frames Production →

C4 addresses
Cheques/POs should be made payable to Channel Four TV Ltd. All requests for leaflets should state programme and episode on envelope. Please allow 28 days for delivery.
1 (programme title)
PO Box 4000
London W3 6XJ
or PO Box 4000
Glasgow G12 9JQ
2 The Open College
Freepost TK1006,
Brentford TW8 8BR

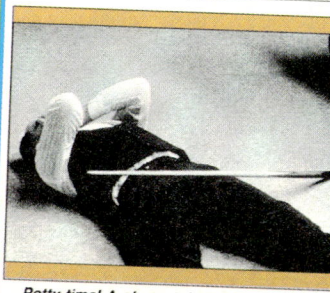

Potty time! A player takes his cue for an unorthodox break in 'The Clydeside Classic'

At a glance

ITV

5.00am	ITN News
6.00	TV-am
9.25	Ghost Train
11.30	The ITV Chart Show
12.30pm	Huckleberry Finn and His Friends
1.00	ITN News
1.05	LWT News
1.10	Saint & Greavsie
1.40	Sportsmasters
2.10	Coronation Street
3.05	Matlock
4.05	Katts and Dog
4.35	Cartoon Time
4.45	Results Service
5.00	ITN News
5.05	LWT News
5.15	Steal
5.45	Baywatch
6.40	Davro
7.10	The Two of Us
7.40	Film: C A T Squad — Stalking Danger
9.35	ITN News and Sport
9.50	LWT Weather
9.55	Aspel & Company
10.40	Tour of Duty
11.40	Film: Carry on Henry
1.25am	Film: Aloha Means Goodbye
3.05	Night Heat
4.05	The Hit Man and Her

Jason Donovan on the 'Ghost Train', 9.25am

C4

6.00am	Early Morning
9.25	Sing & Swing
9.30	Listening Eye
10.00	Film: Vasantha Kokila
12.40pm	The Clydeside Classic
12.50	Film: Captain Boycott
2.40	Channel 4 Racing
5.05	Brookside
6.00	Right to Reply
6.30	Gallery
7.00	The World This Week f/b Weather
8.00	Adventures: Nosey Parker
9.00	thirtysomething
10.00	Film: Landscape in the Mist
12.20am	Yachting
12.50	On the Other Hand
1.50	Film: Feathers
2.45	Close

All TV guides are organised into times and days because this is the way most people organise their lives.

1 Do you sometimes watch television on a Saturday morning? If so, which programmes do you watch?

Which of these two TV guides do you think gives you information about programmes in the most helpful way?

How many different kinds of programme can you identify on these two pages? Make a list of them, copying this chart as a guide. Some of it has been filled in to help you.

Programme type	Examples	Channel
1 News	6.00 News	ITV – LWT
2		
3		
4		
5		
6		

How many of the programmes on these two pages might you be interested in watching? Explain your reasons.

If you were deaf, which programmes might be of particular interest to you?

If you liked indoor games which times of the day might you want to watch the television?

How many films were being shown on the particular Saturday morning shown in the guide? What kinds of films are they?

Often it is not enough just to sort out the major classifications, you need to be more precise. For example you might enjoy cartoons, but hate horror films.

How many different classifications or types of film can you think of? Use the covers of the videos below to help you.

How are video shops organised to help you choose what you want?

Young TV Guide

Design a new kind of *TV Guide* suitable for viewers of your own age.

Stage 1

Find an old *Radio Times* or *TV Times* and bring it into your English lesson.

Stage 2

Decide whether you would like to do this activity individually or in a pair.

Stage 3

Make a list of what you think young people of your own age most want to watch. Use the kinds of headings you were using earlier to classify programmes. Do you and your friends have different tastes? Do they want to see the same amount of each of your classifications?

Stage 4

Do you think it matters what time of day particular programmes are shown? If so, give examples.

Stage 5

Go through your TV guides. Make a note of the programmes you would like to watch. Make another list of those that you think young people might not be so interested in.

Stage 6

Decide how you would improve the way your TV guide is organised. Do you think that it is important to classify it by day and time? Do you think it would be helpful if films and sports were classified in some other way?

Stage 7

Cut out a selection of programmes from your TV guide that you would like to see in your *Young TV Guide*.

Stage 8

Design a day for your *Young TV Guide* using a classifying system that makes it very easy for someone of your own age to use. Remember to make it clear what you have left out.

Stage 9

Make your pages into a class *Young TV Guide*. Bind it properly if possible and try it out on other classes in your school.

Find out how newspapers are classified. What other practical examples can you think of where classifying is important?

Reflection

In this Unit you have been practising how to

- *give a well organised oral account*
- *express your opinions in a group discussion*
- *ask and answer questions in a group*
- *plan and take part in a group presentation*
- *read a children's story aloud*
- *make deductions when you read*
- *argue a point of view about something you have read*
- *show you understand how paragraphs are used*
- *write a children's story*
- *write a poem when you are given the subject*
- *write a guide*

Talk to your friends and your teacher about the things you have been doing in this Unit. Decide how much you have understood and how much progress you have made. Filling in Unit 2 of the Record Sheet on page 44 will also help you think about what you have done in this Unit and the knowledge you are gaining in your English lessons.

Unit 3 Telling Tales

This Unit gives you the opportunity to

- *talk about characters and events*
- *plan your work with a storyboard*
- *tell an oral story*
- *understand different points of view*
- *learn to keep your audience interested*

Storytelling is one of the oldest human pastimes. Before there were books and writing, there were stories. The earliest people must have sat around their fires as night came on and told each other tales they had heard or invented. The tales were remembered and retold. Often they changed and grew in the telling as bits were added to make them more exciting. Many of the oldest stories still survive today and new ones are always being made up. These tales, which are passed on by word of mouth, are called oral stories.

Many oral stories are about a weak but clever hero who outsmarts a strong but stupid villain. The Anansi stories which came originally from Ghana in Africa and later spread all over the Caribbean, are a good example of this. Anansi is a spider who behaves like a man and delights in playing tricks.

1 Divide into small groups. Look at the beginning of this story which tells how Anansi became famous.

How Anansi Became Famous

A long time ago, the Tiger was King of the forest.

At evening when all the animals sat together in a circle and talked and laughed together, Snake would ask: 'Who is the strongest of us all?'

'Tiger is strongest', cried Dog. 'When Tiger whispers the trees listen. When Tiger is angry and cries out, the trees tremble.'

'And who is the weakest of all?' asked Snake.

'Anansi,' shouted Dog, and they all laughed together. 'Anansi the spider is weakest of all. When he whispers no one listens. When he shouts everyone laughs.'

One day the weakest and the strongest came face to face. Anansi and Tiger met in a clearing in the forest. Anansi bowed so low that his forehead touched the ground. 'Good morning, Tiger,' cried Anansi, 'I have a favour to ask.'

'What is it?' said Tiger.

'Tiger, we all know that you are the strongest. That is why we give your name to many things. We have Tiger lilies and Tiger moths, Tiger this and Tiger that. But nothing bears my name. Let something be called after the weakest one, so that men may know my name too.'

'Such as what?' asked the Tiger without so much as a glance towards Anansi.

'The stories,' cried Anansi, 'the stories that we tell in the forest at evening time when the sun goes down.'

Traditional

32

But up to then the stories had always been called Tiger stories. Tiger did not want to change this so he decided to play a trick on Anansi. The trick, of course, backfired.

1 In your groups, think of as many ways as possible in which Tiger could have played a trick on Anansi.

Make a list of all your suggestions.

Decide which one would make the best idea for a story.

Agree how the story goes. You do not need to work it out in detail at this stage.

Split your story up into its main sections. Each group member should take a section.

Now divide into pairs. Each make brief notes on what happens in your section.

Practise telling your section of the story to your partner.

Return to your groups and tell the story once around the group. When you have finished, listen to what other members of the group have to say about the way you told your section.

Tell your story around the group again, this time for the other groups to hear. Try to include any improvements which your own group members have suggested.

Here is a modern oral story. Perhaps you have heard it before. It is not written out in full, just in **storyboard** form. A storyboard is a way of planning out a story using pictures and captions.

1 In pairs, go through this story picture by picture. Work out what you think is happening in the storyboard.

Try telling the story as simply as possible, taking it in turns to describe a picture.

Getting Attention

Which of these possible openings to the storyboard do you prefer and why?

A Hundreds of years ago a woman was walking by the side of a road when ...

B It was a hot summer day when a car pulled up beside the hitch-hiker ...

C I heard a strange story the other day. It concerned a woman who was walking home one day from her village when ...

D Late one night, in a deserted part of the country, a woman was walking home ...

What do you think the first sentence of an oral story should try and do? Which of these do you think works most effectively?

1 AN OLD WOMAN THUMBS A LIFT

2 HOW STRANGE! THE OLD WOMAN WOULDN'T SPEAK. SHE ONLY SHOOK HER HEAD AND NODDED.

BEEN WAITING LONG?

NOT VERY NICE WEATHER FOR HITCHING

3 DRIVER NOTICES HITCH-HIKER'S HANDS. NAILS BROKEN AND DIRTY. HANDS TOO LARGE FOR A WOMAN. HAIRY

4 SHE HAD TO THINK FAST!

COULD YOU CLEAN THE REAR SCREEN FOR ME?

Keeping Your Listeners' Attention

1   Look at picture number 4. Then read out this version of what is happening.

   The driver stopped the car and asked the hitch-hiker to clean the window. The driver drove off as fast as possible.

   Does it hold your attention? Explain your answer carefully. How would you describe this picture if you were trying to keep your listeners as interested as possible?

2   Look at picture number 4 again. Describe this picture from

   a) the driver's point of view
   b) the point of view of the hitch-hiker.

Go through the whole story, telling it from the points of view of both characters.

3   Tell the whole story to a group from your class with the intention of making it as interesting as possible.

   You will need to decide:

   ◆ how important the setting and the time of day are
   ◆ how much to describe each character
   ◆ when to reveal that there is something suspicious about the hitch-hiker
   ◆ on a variety of linking words other than 'then'. (Try to avoid 'And then … '.)

5

6 THE HITCH-HIKER HAD LEFT SOMETHING BEHIND!

7 LOOK WHAT WAS IN IT!

This is a version of an Irish oral story. Take it in turns to read the complete story aloud, either in small groups or in the whole class. You could read a paragraph each.

The Red-Headed Thief

Hundreds and hundreds of years ago in Ireland there lived a man called the Red-Headed Thief. He was called this because he had red hair and because he was a thief. But he wasn't just any old thief. He was the greatest thief in all Ireland, or at least he had been once, when he was a young man. Now he was old and he had not stolen anything for a very long time. All the same he never stopped boasting about what he could steal, if he wanted to.

'I could steal the eye out of a needle,' he used to say. 'I could take the jam out of a sandwich, I could have the steam off your breath – and you'd never even notice.'

One day one of his friends got tired of all this boasting. 'All right then,' he said to the Red-Headed Thief, 'if you're such a great thief, I bet you couldn't steal one of King Conor's horses.'

Now horses were very important at this time, as there were no cars, no buses, no trains, and King Conor's horses were famous throughout the country for being stronger and faster than any other horses. Unfortunately King Conor was also famous throughout all Ireland. He was famous for being nastier, more vicious, and more violent than any other king had ever been.

So when his friend dared him to steal one of King Conor's horses, the Red-Headed Thief thought to himself 'Oh no! What have I said?' but aloud he said, 'Of course I could.'

'Go on then,' said his friend.

'What, now?' said the Red-Headed Thief.

'Yes now,' said his friend.

So there and then the Red-Headed Thief set off to try and steal one of King Conor's horses. He travelled all day long and by nightfall he reached King Conor's palace.

Because he really was such a skilful thief he had no difficulty slipping past the soldiers on guard. He quickly found the stables and ducked inside. There he found the three horses of King Conor. They were magnificent animals and the Red-Headed Thief paused for a moment just to gaze at them. Then he put out his hand to stroke the nearest horse. But as soon as he touched it the horse began neighing and kicking furiously. The Red-Headed Thief tried to calm it down but it was no good. Before you could snap your fingers he found himself surrounded by guards who seized him and dragged him away to the throne-room.

King Conor was sitting on his throne. He was a savage and ugly man. Sitting next to him was his wife, an equally savage and even uglier woman. In front of them was a fire and on the fire was a large black cauldron, full of oil. The oil was hissing and sizzling. The Red-Headed Thief did not like the look of it at all.

When King Conor saw the Red-Headed Thief he smiled. 'So,' he said, 'you were trying to steal one of my horses, eh?'

'Yes, your majesty,' the Red-Headed Thief stammered.

'Do you know what I'm going to do with you?' King Conor asked.

'No, your majesty,' the Red-Headed Thief replied, though he had a very good idea.

'I'm going to throw you into that cauldron of boiling oil,' King Conor told him. He gave a horrible smile as he said this and looked at the queen, his wife. She smiled back at him and rubbed her hands together.

King Conor was a man who enjoyed his moments of power. He liked to draw them out, to savour them. So he said to the Red-Headed Thief, 'I bet you've never in all your life been closer to death than you are now.'

If there was one thing the Red-Headed Thief was good at, it was thinking: thinking fast, thinking on his feet. So he said to King Conor, 'Well actually, since you ask, I have come nearer to death than I am now.'

'Oh really?' said King Conor. 'When was that?'

'Well, it's a long story. You are just about to boil me alive. Let's not bother about it now,' the Red-Headed Thief replied.

'Do as I say!' commanded King Conor. 'Tell me when and how you came nearer to death than you are now.'

'All right, if you insist,' said the Red-Headed Thief, and he began to speak of what the world was like when he was a young man.

In those days, he said, he travelled the length and breadth of Ireland looking for things to steal and in his travels he came across many places that others didn't even know existed. One day when he was walking down a deserted country lane he suddenly found himself in front of the biggest mansion he had ever seen. 'Bigger than your palace, King Conor,' the Red-Headed Thief said.

King Conor looked annoyed at this but he said nothing.

And sitting on a rock outside this huge mansion, the Red-Headed Thief told them, was a young woman. She was sitting on the rock and sobbing. The tears were rolling down her cheeks.

Cradled in her left arm, she had a baby and all the time the young woman was crying the baby kept laughing and laughing. In her right hand she held a very long, very sharp kitchen knife. She kept bringing the knife to just within a whisker of the baby's throat, then taking it away again, then putting it back, over and over again. All the time that she did this the baby kept laughing and chortling but the young woman kept crying and crying and the tears were rolling down her cheeks.

The Red-Headed Thief thought this was very strange so he went up to her and asked her why she was crying.

'I'm crying,' she told him, 'because I'm going to be eighteen tomorrow.'

'Well that's nothing to cry about,' said the Red-Headed Thief. 'Happy birthday!'

'No, you don't understand,' the young woman said. 'A year ago I was at a fair with my mother, my father, my brothers and sisters. There was nobody in all Ireland happier than me. Then all of a sudden into the fair burst three giants. Well, everybody was so amazed to see them that those who were in the middle of eating stopped with the food half way to their mouths, those who were in the middle of drinking stopped with the cup half way to their lips, and those who were in the middle of a conversation stopped what they were saying. Everybody stood and stared as the three giants robbed them of everything they had. Then they picked me up, brought me to this place and told me I was to marry the eldest of the giants. I told them I couldn't because I was too young. So they said I was to wait until I was old enough and tomorrow I will be eighteen and I'll have to marry the eldest of the giants.'

The Red-Headed Thief whistled to himself. 'That's bad,' he said. 'But tell me, what is the baby that you have cradled in your left arm and why do you keep bringing that knife to its throat and then taking it away again, over and over again?'

'That's even worse,' the young woman said. 'You see the giants have all gone to work, but before they left they brought me this baby and told me to kill it, to cook it and to put it in a pie for their tea but I can't bring myself to do it.'

The Red-Headed Thief sighed. It was certainly a difficult problem, but if there was one thing he was good at it was thinking: thinking fast, thinking on his feet. Suddenly he had an idea. 'Listen,' he said to the young woman, 'I've got a pig. Why don't we kill that and put it in the pie instead of the baby?'

'No, that's no good,' the young woman replied.

'Isn't it?' said the Red-Headed Thief.

'Of course not,' she told him. 'They'll know it isn't the baby.'

'I suppose so,' the Red-Headed Thief said. He thought for a little bit longer, then he said. 'I've got it! This is what we do: we kill the pig, like I suggested, then we take the baby and cut the tip of its little finger off. We put the pig in the pie with the tip of the baby's little finger and we give it to the giants. When they find the tip of the baby's little finger they'll think it's the baby in the pie. What do you think?'

'Ugh!' said the young woman, 'that's disgusting.'

'Well have you got a better idea?' asked the Red-Headed Thief.

The young woman didn't have a better idea so, in the end, that was what they did. They killed the pig, cut the tip of the baby's little finger off, put them both in a pie together and put the pie in the oven. It was very nearly cooked when the Red-Headed Thief heard a terrible thumping noise.

'What's that?' he said.

'Oh that's just the giants coming home from work,' the young woman told him.

'Just the giants!' the Red-Headed Thief said. He looked around for somewhere to hide. He couldn't see anywhere and the thumping was getting louder. So he rushed into the giant's house and hid in the kitchen.

Home came the giants. 'Where's our supper?' they asked the young woman. She took the pie out of the oven and brought it to them. As she did so she thought to herself, 'They'll know it's not the baby.' But they didn't know. They each cut themselves a slice and tucked in. Halfway through the meal one of the giants put his hand to his mouth, pulled out the tip of the baby's finger and looked at it. 'You should cut the meat up properly,' he told the young woman, and threw it into the fire.

After the meal the giants sat around for a while. Then one of them said, 'That was very nice, but I'm still hungry. I think I'll go and see if there's anything else to eat in the kitchen.'

When the Red-Headed Thief heard this he looked around for somewhere to hide. But there was nowhere. He could hear the giant getting closer and closer. 'What am I going to do?' he thought to himself. But if there was one thing he was good at, it was thinking: thinking fast, thinking on his feet. Just as the giant opened the door, the Red-Headed Thief had an idea. He lay down on the kitchen table and pretended to be dead.

Now this would have been a very good idea if the giant had not taken one look at him and said to himself, 'Ah, that's just what I fancy to eat!'

He walked over to the table, picked up the very long, very sharp kitchen knife and cut a big piece off the Red-Headed Thief's left leg.

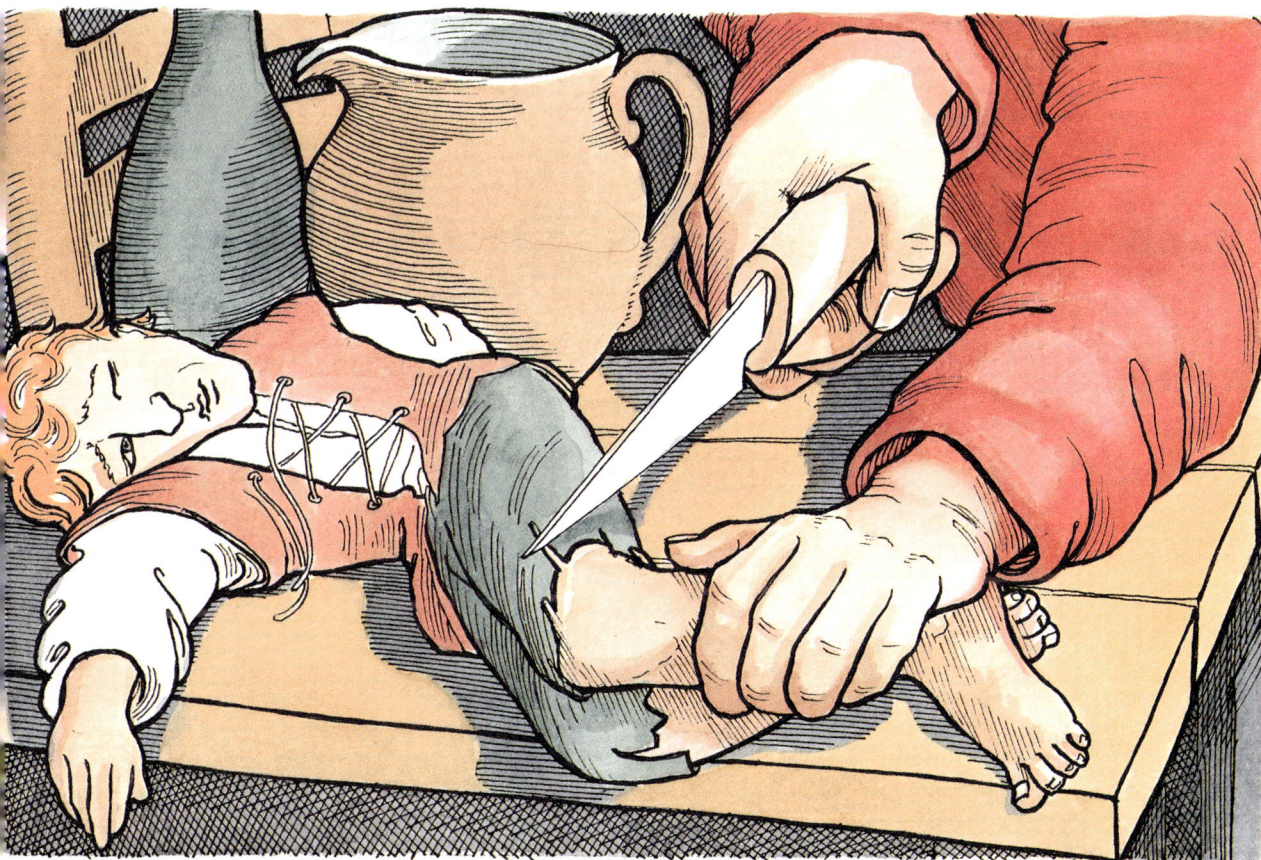

The pain was terrible but the Red-Headed Thief was supposed to be dead. So he couldn't cry out. The giant turned and began to walk out with a piece of the Red-Headed Thief's leg in his hand. Somehow, despite the terrible wound in his leg, the Red-Headed Thief stumbled down off the table, seized the very long, very sharp kitchen knife and plunged it into the giant's back. The giant fell down dead.

Blood was pouring from the Red-Headed Thief's leg but he bent down and began to drag the body of the dead giant out of the way behind the door. He had just got it hidden when he heard the second giant say 'That was very nice, but I'm still hungry. I think I'll go and see if there's anything else to eat in the kitchen.'

'What am I going to do?' thought the Red-Headed Thief. By now he wasn't thinking too well at all. He could hear the giant's footsteps getting closer and closer. Just as the giant opened the door, he got back onto the kitchen table and lay down, pretending to be dead.

The giant took one look at him and said to himself, 'Ah, that's just what I fancy to eat!'

He walked over to the table, picked up the very long, very sharp kitchen knife and cut a big piece off the Red-Headed Thief's right leg.

The pain was terrible but the Red-Headed Thief was supposed to be dead. So he couldn't cry out. The giant turned and began to walk out with a piece of the Red-Headed Thief's leg in his hand. Somehow, despite the terrible wound in his leg, the Red-Headed Thief stumbled down off the table, seized the very long, very sharp kitchen knife and plunged it into the giant's back. The giant fell down dead.

Blood was pouring from both the Red-Headed Thief's legs but he bent down and began to drag the body of the dead giant out of the way behind the door. He was very weak from his terrible wounds and he was still struggling when he looked up and saw, towering over him, the figure of the third giant.

This was the eldest of the giants, the strongest and the meanest. He didn't say a word when he saw the Red-Headed Thief bending over the body of his dead brother. He just raised his club above his head and brought it crashing to the ground.

The Red-Headed Thief managed to move to one side just in time. He seized the very long, very sharp kitchen knife and plunged it into the giant's side. But the giant didn't die. Instead he gave a bellow of anger and brought the club crashing down on the Red-Headed Thief. Again the Red-Headed Thief just managed to dodge the blow. He plunged the knife into the giant's other side but still the giant would not die. He raised his club a third time and brought it down on the Red-Headed Thief. This time he caught him a glancing blow and tore a big piece out of the Red-Headed Thief's side.

The Red-Headed Thief was very nearly dead himself now, but summoning up all his strength, he plunged the knife into the giant's belly. The third giant fell down dead.

There they lay in a great grisly heap, the three dead giants. The Red-Headed Thief fell down on top of them. In came the young woman. 'Red-Headed Thief,' she said. 'You've killed the giants, you've saved the baby's life and saved me from a horrible fate. You're wonderful!'

'Yes, I know,' said the Red-Headed Thief 'and now I'm going to die, but it's been worth it.'

'No, you don't have to die,' said the young woman. 'The giants have got a cauldron of cure.'

'A cauldron of cure? What's that?' said the Red-Headed Thief.

'It's a magic cauldron,' said the young woman. 'It will cure all your wounds.'

'But I'm too weak to find it,' said the Red-Headed Thief.

'Don't worry,' said the young woman, 'I'll carry you there.'

So she picked up the Red-Headed Thief and began to carry him to the cauldron of cure. All the time she was carrying him the Red-Headed Thief was dying. His breathing was growing weaker and weaker. The world was growing colder and colder, darker and darker. Now all he could see in front of him was a narrow tunnel of light and the tunnel was growing smaller and smaller until it was just a pinprick of light. The Red-Headed Thief was breathing his last as the young woman lowered him into the cauldron.

Instantly he was cured! All his wounds were healed. He was perfectly well again.

'And that,' said the Red-Headed Thief to King Conor, 'was the time I was nearer death than I am now. You must admit I was nearer death that time.'

King Conor said nothing but his wife said, 'Magic cauldron! Giants! It's rubbish! He's making it up. Go on, boil him in oil, that's the bit I want to see.'

But King Conor raised his hand and said, 'Silence!' and everybody in the palace was silent. Everybody in the palace was silent because they had just noticed something for the first time. What they had just noticed was that when King Conor raised his hand and said 'Silence!' the tip of his little finger was missing.

'Oh no, it's not rubbish!' said King Conor. 'I know because I was that baby and I've been looking for the person who saved my life ever since. Far from boiling you in oil, Red-Headed Thief, I would like to offer you a reward. Is there anything I can give you for saving my life all those years ago?'

'Well, your highness,' said the Red-Headed Thief. 'There is one little thing.'

'Name it,' said King Conor.

'If I could just borrow one of your horses ... ' the Red-Headed Thief said.

'Of course,' said King Conor. 'Take it.'

So then and there the Red-Headed Thief went down to the stables, saddled one of King Conor's horses and rode all night until he got back to his house where his friends were waiting. 'There you are,' he told them. 'I told you I could steal one of King Conor's horses. It was easy.'

Traditional

1 In groups, look at these statements and decide which you agree with.

It is obvious from the beginning what will happen to the Red-Headed Thief.

It is obvious that the baby will turn out to be King Conor.

It is only near the end that you realise that the baby will turn out to be King Conor.

The Red-Headed Thief had never met King Conor before.

The Red-Headed Thief made the whole story up when he noticed that the tip of King Conor's finger was missing.

The Red-Headed Thief escaped because King Conor's wife took pity on him.

Can you think of any statement of your own to add?

In fact, most listeners do not guess how the story will end. This is because the way the story is told keeps the listener in suspense for as long as possible. There are a number of ways of creating interest in a story.

2 In pairs, look carefully at these words from the story.

'I could steal the eye out of a needle,' he used to say. 'I could take the jam out of a sandwich, I could have the steam off your breath ... '

Now horses were very important at this time, as there were no cars, no buses, no trains ...

King Conor's horses were famous throughout the country for being stronger and faster than any other horses. Unfortunately King Conor was also famous throughout all Ireland. He was famous for being nastier, more vicious, and more violent than any other king had ever been.

King Conor was sitting on his throne. He was a savage and ugly man. Sitting next to him was his wife, an equally savage and even uglier woman.

If there was one thing the Red-Headed Thief was good at, it was thinking: thinking fast, thinking on his feet.

those who were in the middle of eating stopped with the food half way to their mouths, those who were in the middle of drinking stopped with the cup half way to their lips, and those who were in the middle of a conversation stopped what they were saying.

What do you notice about the way that words are used in these extracts?

People who tell stories like these do so from memory. How might this help them?

What effect does the repetition of words or groups of words have on you, when you listen to the story?

Repetition of words or groups of words is one of the common elements in most oral stories. Here are some other common elements which, when used together, help to create interest.

◆ Planting an idea early in the story which can be used at the end to create a surprise. For example, in *The Red-Headed Thief* the tip of the baby's finger is cut off in the middle of the story. You forget about this until the very end.

◆ Telling a story within the story.

◆ Repeated actions, for example, the three giants coming into the kitchen.

◆ Matters of life and death (oral stories are often quite bloodthirsty!)

◆ Magical items.

In a group again, find as many examples of each of the features as you can in the story. You have been given some help above.

Plan and Record your Own Oral Story

You are going to make up a story about a surprising near escape from death, suitable for telling to your class.

Stage 1

Decide on your main character. It could be the Red-Headed Thief or a character of your own choice.

Stage 2

Decide what it is about your character that makes him or her special.

Stage 3

Make up a villain who will put your character in danger.

Stage 4

Choose a situation in which they meet.

Stage 5

Decide how your character will escape.

Stage 6

Make a storyboard like the one you studied about the hitch-hiker, but don't worry if your drawings are very simple!

Stage 7

In pairs try out your stories on each other.

Stage 8

Listen to each others' comments and make any improvements that you can.

Stage 9

Tape-record your story.

A story like this takes a lot of remembering. Practise telling your story to each other. Go back to the tape if you forget where you are. When you have learnt the story off by heart you could organise a storytelling festival in which you perform to another class or classes.

Reflection

In this Unit you have been practising how to

- *plan and tell an oral story*
- *read a story aloud with expression*
- *talk about characters and events in stories*
- *read and listen to oral stories*
- *produce a storyboard*

Talk to your friends and your teacher about the things you have been doing in this Unit. Decide how much you have understood and how much progress you have made. Filling in Unit 3 of the Record Sheet on page 44 will also help you think about what you have done in this Unit and the knowledge you are gaining in your English lessons.

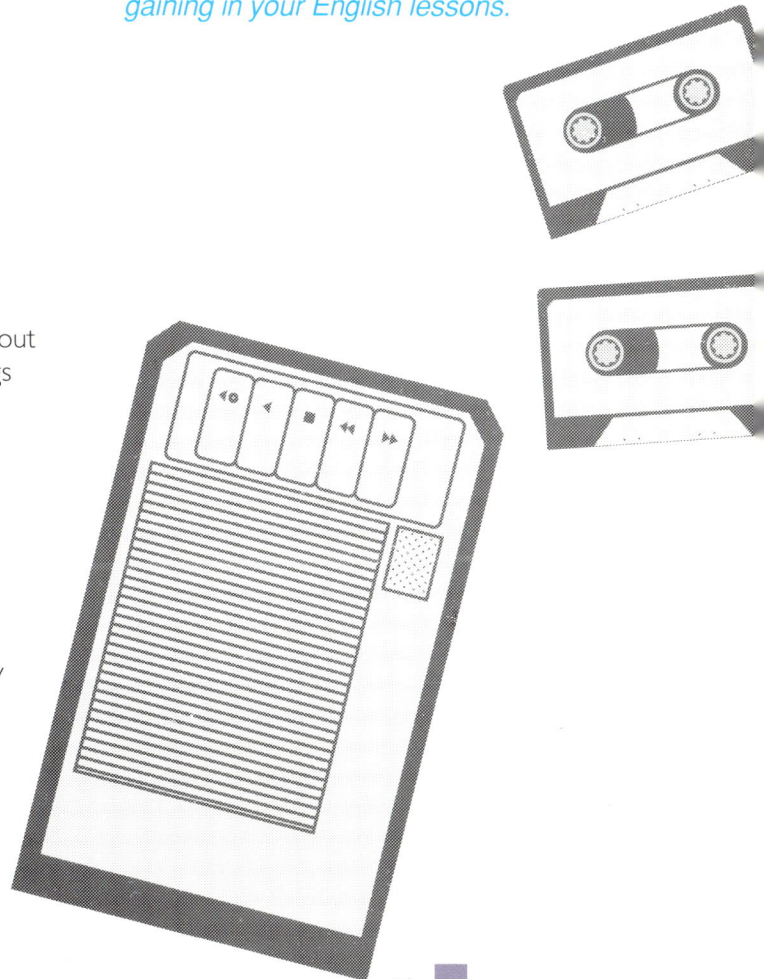

Important: Your teacher will give you photocopied versions of these two pages so that you do not need to write in this book.

First of all, with a friend, talk about and decide what the short statements mean. Discuss what you have been practising in English and how much you have understood of what you have done.

Next to each statement there are three targets to aim for. This is what they mean:

I understand this and have practised it.

I have done this with help.

I feel able to do this again.

If you are not sure what a statement means or whether you can do what it says, discuss it with your teacher.

Put a tick under the target that you think best describes what you can do. If you are in doubt, please ask for help.

Name of Student

I can

Unit 1
- talk about characters and events in stories
- read and listen to oral stories
- produce a storyboard

Unit 2
- show understanding of how paragraphs are used
- write a children's story
- write a poem from a given subject
- write a guide
- plan and tell an oral story
- read a story aloud with expression

Unit 3
- talk about dialect
- talk about some differences between spoken and Standard English
- talk about characters and events in stories
- set out speech in a story
- write a story for a given audience
- use the apostrophe
- give a well-organised oral account
- express my opinion in a group discussion
- ask and answer questions in a group
- plan and take part in a group presentation
- read a children's story aloud
- make deductions when reading
- argue a point of view about something I have read

			Other comments

Thinking Back

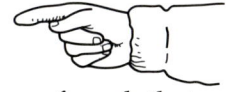

◆ Which is the best piece of work that you have done so far? Why do you think it was particularly successful?

◆ Which of the work in the last three Units did you enjoy most?

◆ What have you learned about language that you did not know before?

◆ Was there anything you did not understand and would like more help with?

Thinking Forward

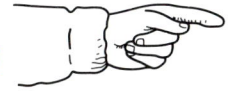

◆ Where do you think you need to improve most? What can you do to help you do so?

◆ What kind of activities can you suggest to your teacher that you could do as extra work?

This Unit gives you the opportunity to

- *express your feelings about poems*
- *ask and answer questions*
- *read a range of poetry*
- *take part in a presentation*
- *draft a poem*
- *make an anthology*

1 Read this poem which was written for a special edition of posters with photographs of animals on them. Each of the animals shown on the posters is in some way in danger of becoming extinct.

Orang Utan

Watch me,
touch me,
catch-me-if-you-can!
I am
soundless,
swung-from-your-sight,
gone with the wind,
shiver of air,
trick-of-the-light.

Watch me,
touch me,
catch-me-if-you-dare!
I hide, I glide,
I stride through air,
shatter the day-star dappled light
over forest floor.
The world's in my grasp!
I am windsong,
sky-flier,
man-of-the-woods,
the arm of the law.

Judith Nicholls

2 In pairs, read the poem aloud to each other. What impression of an orang utan does the poem give you?

Look at the photograph. What impression does it create of an orang utan? Which do you prefer?

Choose two or three lines from the poem that you think best describe the orang utan.

What do you think 'the arm of the law' means? Why do you think Judith Nicholls uses this to describe an orang utan?

Making a Poem

Most poets go through several stages before the final poem is produced.

This is what Judith Nicholls, a professional poet, said about how she writes a poem.

Judith Nicholls, how do you start writing a poem?

Usually in minor panic at the sight of a blank sheet of paper. For me, the blank sheet of paper is the hardest part of all and I like to force myself to get something onto it as quickly as possible. Staring at it for too long merely increases the panic!

Many of the poems I write begin now as responses to requests for other people's anthologies and I find this a good discipline. A letter requesting poems on this or that is rather like having a teacher demanding work on some subject in which I may (initially) have little interest – or knowledge!

How many stages does a typical Judith Nicholls poem go through? Could you describe each stage carefully for the benefit of younger poets?

As with the Orang Utan poem, I tend to start by scribbling down any idea at all that comes to me initially. These ideas may come from looking closely, touching, listening, maybe smelling or even tasting (I have written one poem called 'How to eat a strawberry')! Some of the first ideas may seem quite good sense (for example, the orang utan as a gymnast on ropes), others may seem pretty crazy (a Christmas tree fairy!) but it's important to remember that when we start writing none of the ideas are 'right' or 'wrong'. Starting like this with a completely open mind can uncover some surprising ideas sometimes.

After this brainstorming I will probably go on to any research that's needed. I enjoy this part; it's panic-free and I can feel I'm doing something constructive! This session can also uncover some interesting information that I may want to use (for example, orang utan is a Malay word meaning 'old man of the forest').

When I have gathered plenty of ideas and information I concentrate on making the poem. 'Making' really means 'crafting': I want to arrange, twist, bend, pummel, select, discard, play with the basic material until I have got it as I want it. I nearly always throw out words as well as change and rearrange. In a poem each word should be doing a useful job. I say it aloud (most important to check the music of the poem) change it, scribble it out again, leave it another day, say it aloud again, change another word ... often fourteen or fifteen drafts. It's a messy business.

1 Here are just three of the many drafts Judith
Nicholls made for the poem about the orang
utan. Look at them carefully. Find the words she
talks about in her answers.

4

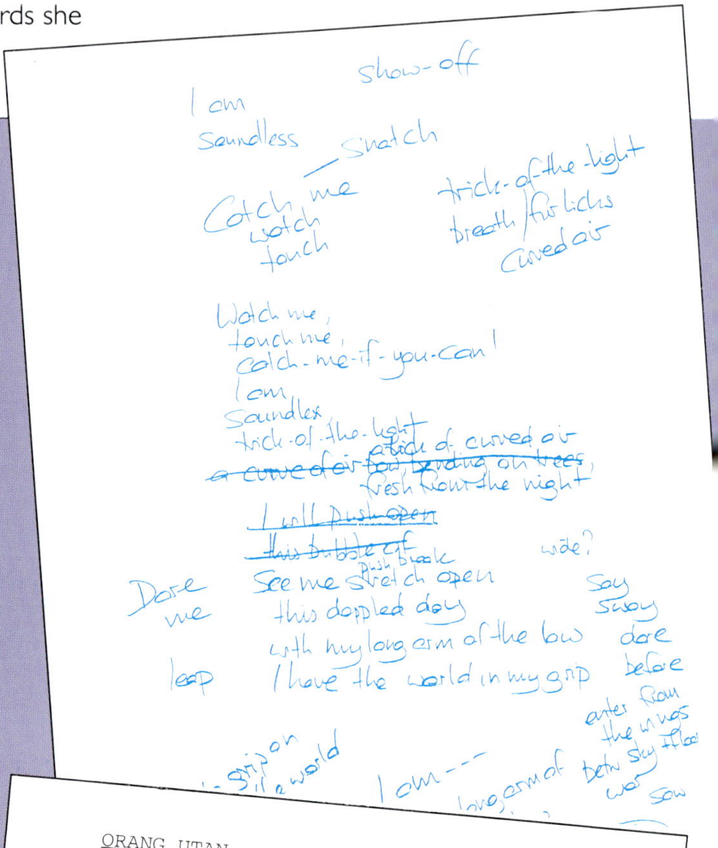

(handwritten draft notes)

show-off

I am
soundless   snatch

Catch me   trick-of-the-light
    watch   breath/frolics
    touch   curved air

Watch me,
touch me,
catch-me-if-you-can!
I am
soundless
trick-of-the-light
a curve of air too ~~young in trees~~
                   track of curved air
                   fresh from the night

I will ~~push open~~
~~this bubble of~~
                 ~~fresh break~~   wide?

Dare   See me stretch open   say
me   this dappled day   sway
            with my long arm of the bow   dare
leap   I have the world in my grip   before
                                                after from
                                                the winds
                        ... in   the sky floor
                         ... a world   war
                                              sow
I am---
         long arm of

1

(handwritten draft notes)

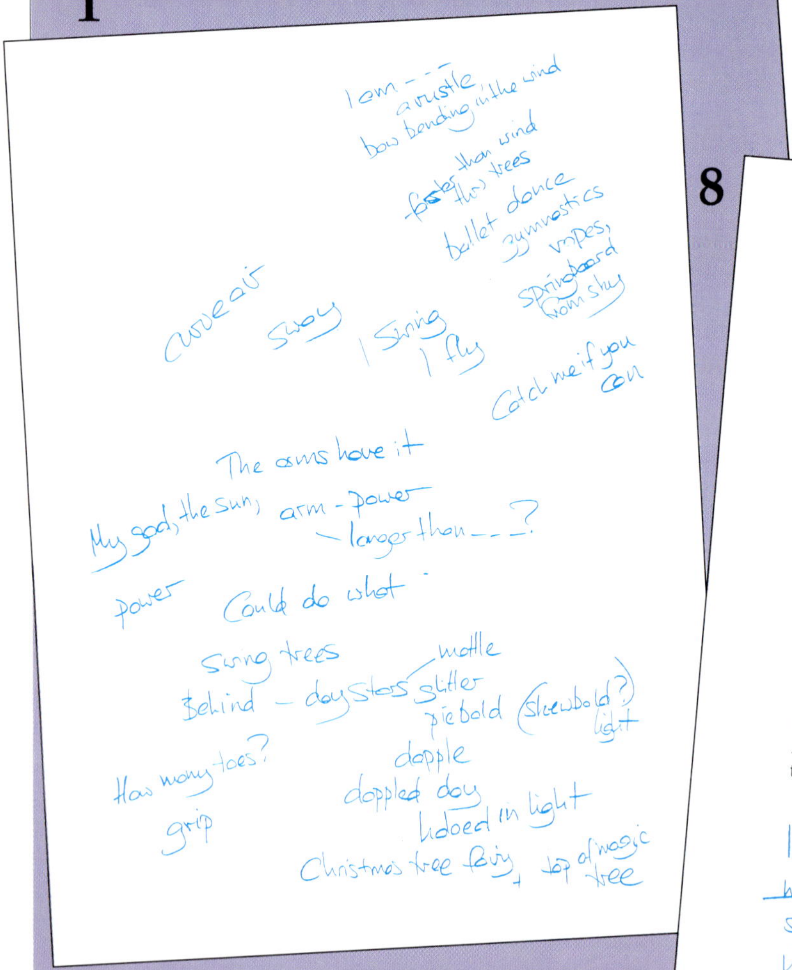

I am---
        a rustle
bow bending in the wind
        faster than wind
                   the trees
        ballet dance
                 gymnastics
                         ropes,
                      springboard
                      (from sky)
curved air   sway   I swing
                         I fly
                              Catch me if you
                                      can

The arms have it
My god, the sun)   arm-power
                      – larger than---?
power   Could do what

Swing trees   wattle
Behind – day-stars stiller
                   piebald (skewbald?)
                                 light
How many toes?   dapple
                  dappled day
grip   hidden in light
         Christmas tree fairy, top of magic tree

8

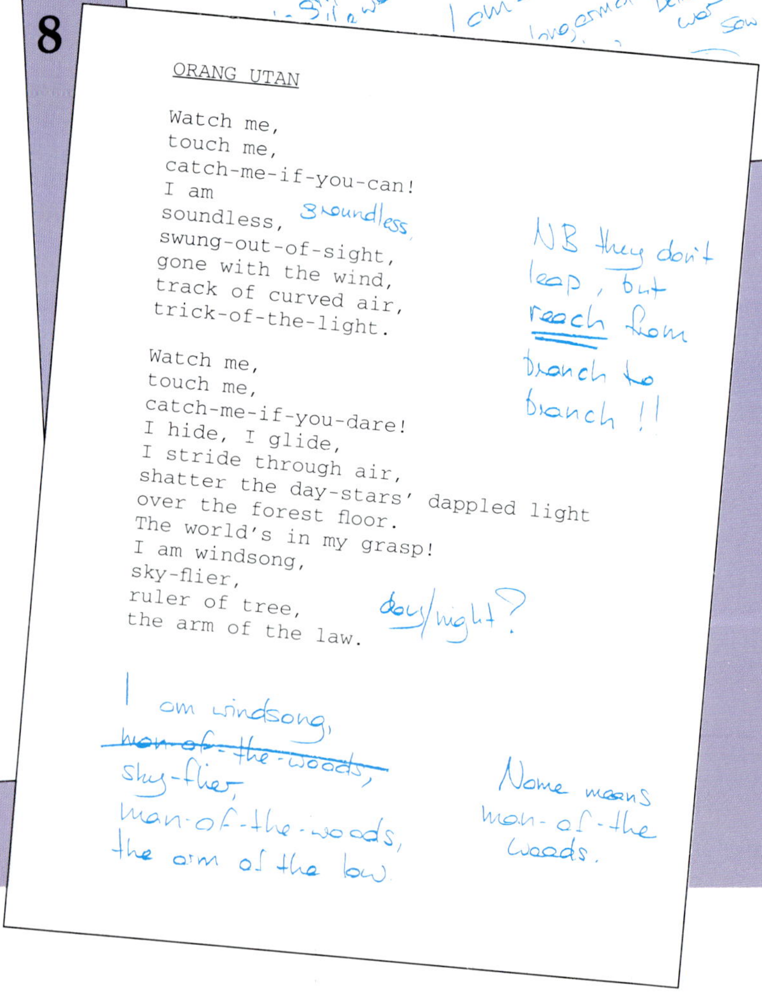

ORANG UTAN

Watch me,
touch me,
catch-me-if-you-can!
I am
soundless,   *soundless,*
swung-out-of-sight,
gone with the wind,
track of curved air,
trick-of-the-light.

Watch me,
touch me,
catch-me-if-you-dare!
I hide, I glide,
I stride through air,
shatter the day-stars' dappled light
over the forest floor.
The world's in my grasp!
I am windsong,
sky-flier,
ruler of tree,   *day/night?*
the arm of the law.

*NB they don't
leap , but
reach from
branch to
branch !!*

I am windsong,
~~*man-of-the-woods,*~~
sky-flier,
man-of-the-woods,
the arm of the law

*Name means
man-of-the-
woods.*

2   Which ideas from her first draft does Judith Nicholls cut out later?

Which line has she changed between the third draft shown here and her final poem? Which version do you prefer?

3   Write a poem about an animal which is an endangered species, to go with a photograph of your choice. Aim your poem at people of your own age, who do not necessarily know that the animal is in danger.

Follow the stages Judith Nicholls describes in her answers.

Starting Writing

Think about what you have been asked to do. On a blank page or wordprocessor screen 'brainstorm' any ideas that come into your head. This might take the form of a list of words, a diagram or notes.

It might help to do some research in your school library. Find out which animals are currently in danger and choose one to write about. Select a possible photograph to work with. If you prefer, you can leave this until later in the process.

Composing

Concentrate on 'crafting' your poem. You will need to decide what kind of poem you are going to write.

Revising

Start to 'play' with your ideas. Try out your words and lines. Arrange them on the page or screen. Try reading them aloud to a friend. Listen to any comments your friend makes which you find helpful. At this stage you might like to make changes to your poem. Don't worry about neatness too much.

Leave it for a day. Show it to someone else. Put it beside your photograph and see if you think of any more ideas.

Proof-reading

Check your spelling and punctuation. Use your dictionary. You might like to write your poem out again to make it clearer.

Publishing

Decide how you are going to present it in its final form. Again, it might help to leave your poem for a day or show it to someone else. Then produce your final draft.

The poems on these pages are presented as they might appear in an anthology or collection of poetry produced for young people. They are there to be enjoyed first. If you want to develop your ideas about some of these poems further, some activities follow on page 59.

Tropical Dream

At times like this when I sit alone
My memories I recall,
Of a time when I was just a boy,
Of a land that was my joy.
Of mountain tops that seemed so high,
Of rivers deep and wide,
Of great big ships their anchors drawn
Just waiting for the tide.

The burning sun would shine all day,
The skies were never grey.
The birds would sing their songs so gay
As they flew from tree to tree.
At times I'd sit in a shaded glade
And watch them at their play.
It was a beautiful sight to see
On a bright and sunny day.

In the evening when my chores were done,
My books I'd set aside.
Through woodland parks I'd stroll alone
Exploring far and wide.
The smell of flowers would fill the air,
I would whistle as I walked,
And in a distance loud and clear
Some howling dog would bark.

The setting sun was to the west
As the evening turned to night.
That's when the sky was at its best
With stars that shone so bright.
The moon it seemed to me so big,
Surrounded by the stars,
While on the veranda I would sit
As my uncle played his guitar.

It's all so clear as if it were just only yesterday,
That I was just another boy who cherished everyday.
It's just a dream, a poet's dream
And one day soon to come
I will return no more to roam.

Errol Wynter

The Moth

The moth is a fat, stubby glider;
Its wedge-shaped wings of blotchy rose-petal
Flutter madly,
Almost too madly to be graceful.
But it is,
As it flits and hovers,
Like a dandelion clock caught in an unsteady breeze.

Its body is a cream eclair,
Ready to split at the slightest squeeze.
Its eyes are tiny
Pinheads on a tight bundle of rags,
Pushed down in the toe of an old stocking.
And its legs aren't legs;
They are runners – Not for walking,
But hanging and standing.

The moth is a crippled angel.
It worships light,
As if it were a god; it stays with it,
Rarely leaving.
But the moth is an insect,
A soldier of fortune.
And a new battle for survival
Dawns every day.

Stephen Gardam (12)

The Spider

The spider, a mistake
On God's paper.
A thumb print of ink
That splattered eight ways.
He hides guiltily in shadows,
And scurries, face lowered.
He's accused of a crime
That he didn't commit.
The crime is life,
So he hides away from it,
And takes revenge
On content thieves
That stole freedom.
But he is a spider,
A mistake on God's paper.
A mistake never to be forgiven.

Thea Smiley (13)

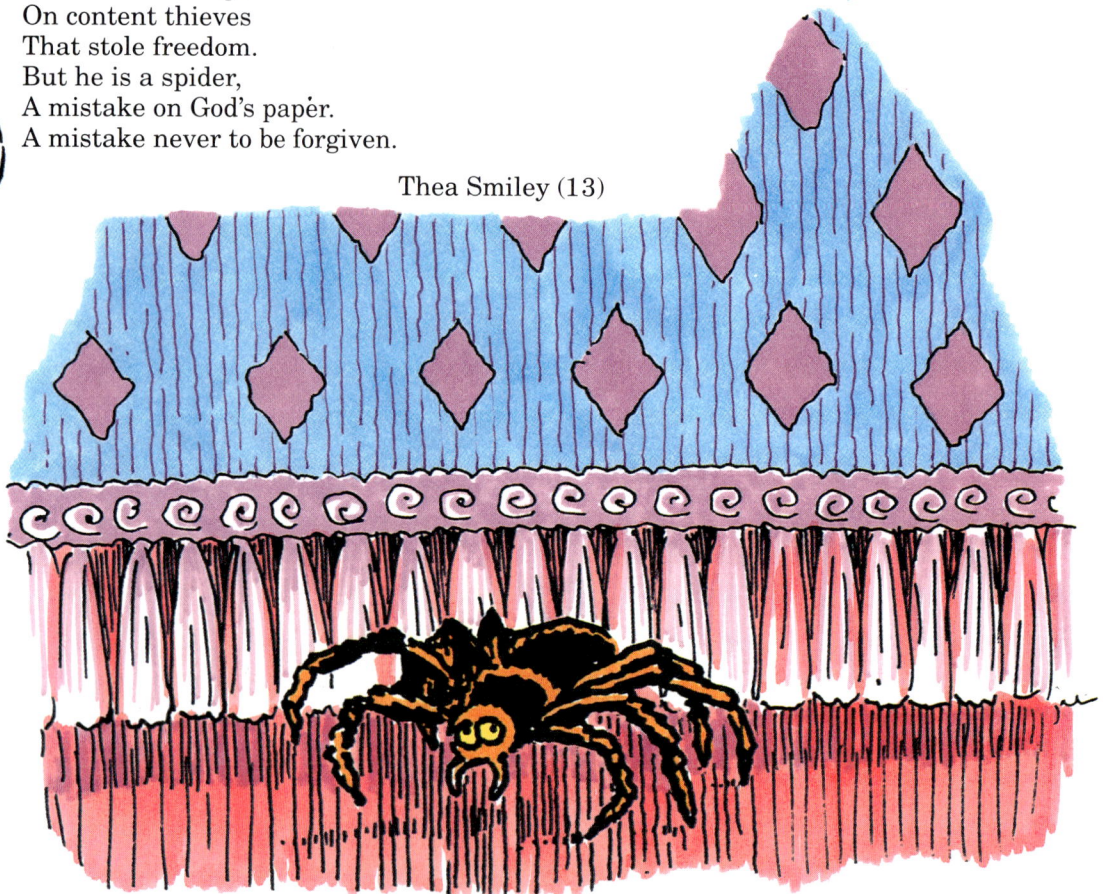

This is Just to Say

This is just to say
I have eaten
the plums
that were in
the icebox

and which
you were probably
saving
for breakfast

Forgive me
they were delicious
so sweet
and so cold

William Carlos Williams

Raw Carrots

Raw carrots taste
Cool and hard,
Like some crisp metal.

Horses are
Fond of them,
Crunching up

The red gold
With much wet
Juice and noise.

Carrots must taste
To horses
As they do to us.

Valerie Worth

The Song of the Homeworkers

To be read or chanted with increasing velocity

Homework moanwork
Cross it out and groanwork
Homework neatwork
Keeps you off the streetwork
Homework moanwork
Cross it out and groanwork
Homework roughwork
When you've had enoughwork
Homework moanwork
Cross it out and groanwork
Homework dronework
Do it on your ownwork
Homework moanwork
Cross it out and groanwork

Homework gloomwork
Gaze around the roomwork
Homework moanwork
Cross it out and groanwork
Homework guesswork
Book is in a messwork
Homework moanwork
Cross it out and groanwork
Homework rushwork
Do it on the buswork
Homework moanwork
Cross it out and groanwork
Homework hatework
Hand your book in latework
Homework moanwork
Cross it out and groan groan GROANWORK

Trevor Millum

The Car Trip

Mum says:
'Right, you two,
this is a very long car journey.
I want you two to be good.
I'm driving and I can't drive properly
if you two are going mad in the back.
Do you understand?'

So we say,
'OK, Mum, OK. Don't worry,'
and off we go.

And we start The Moaning:
Can I have a drink?
I want some crisps.
Can I open my window?
He's got my book.
Get off me.
Ow, that's my ear!

And Mum tries to be exciting:
'Look out the window
there's a lamp-post.'

And we go on with The Moaning:
Can I have a sweet?
He's sitting on me.
Are we nearly there?
Don't scratch.
You never tell him off.
Now he's biting his nails.
I want a drink. I want a drink.

And Mum tries to be exciting again:
'Look out the window
There's a tree.'

And we go on:
My hands are sticky.
He's playing with the doorhandle now.
I feel sick.
Your nose is all runny.
Don't pull my hair.
He's punching me, Mum,
that's really dangerous, you know.
Mum, he's spitting.

And Mum says:
'Right I'm stopping the car.
I AM STOPPING THE CAR.'

She stops the car.

'Now, if you two don't stop it
I'm going to put you out of the car
and leave you by the side of the road.'

He started it.
I didn't. He started it.

'I don't care who started it
I can't drive properly
if you two go mad in the back.
Do you understand?'

And we say:
OK. Mum, OK, don't worry.

Can I have a drink?

Mike Rosen

55

You have already had a chance to find out how a professional poet makes her poems. Judith Nicholls is also the editor of an anthology of poetry called *What on Earth ...?* In this interview the same poet was asked how she went about choosing poems for this book.

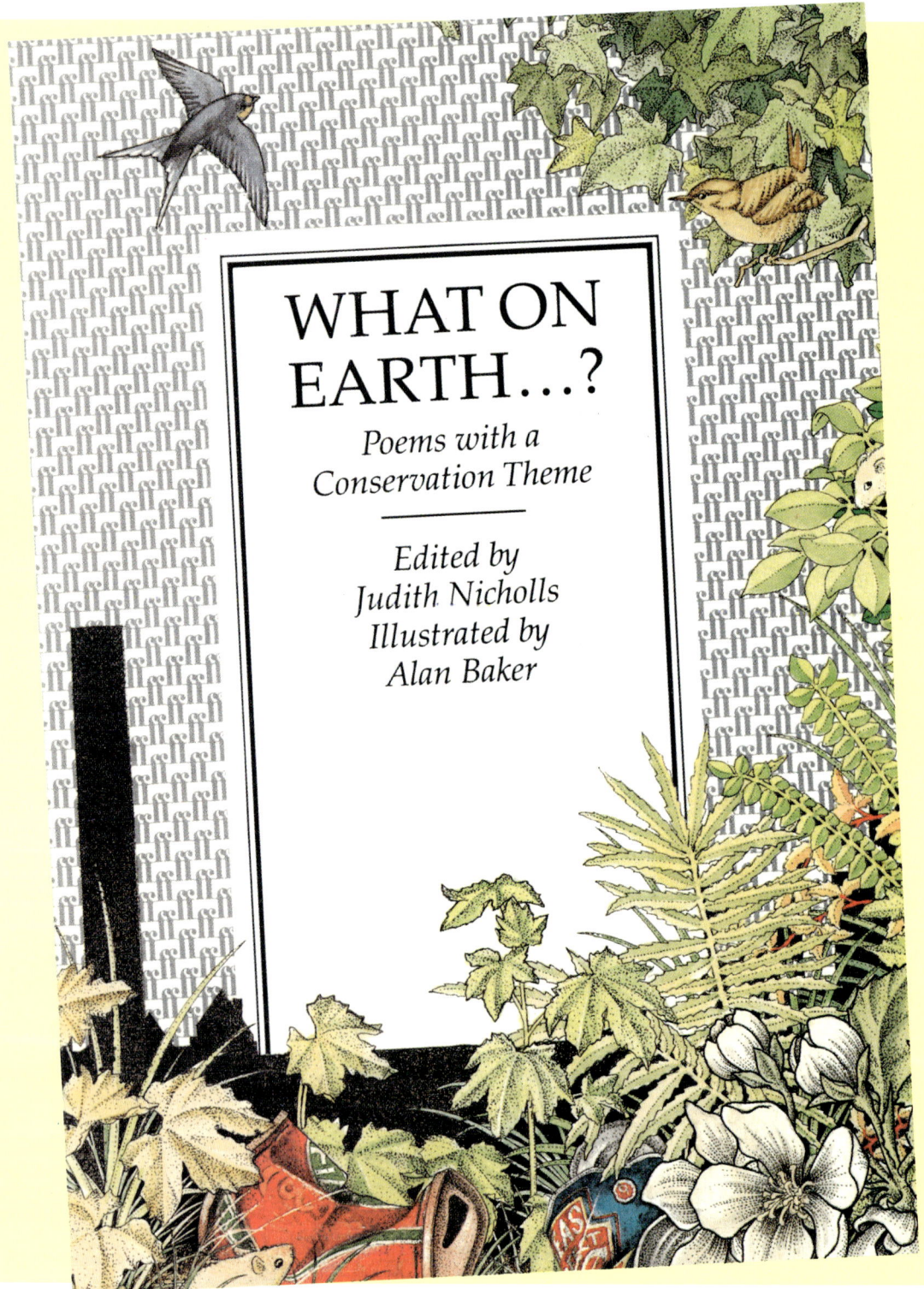

WHAT ON EARTH...?

Poems with a Conservation Theme

Edited by Judith Nicholls Illustrated by Alan Baker

Interview with Judith Nicholls

How did you go about making your poetry anthology *What on Earth ...??*

I'd compiled a poetry programme of conservation poems for BBC's *Living Language* and realised there appeared to be few around at the time. It seemed to be a good idea for an anthology. I gathered what I could and spent hours reading poetry books at home and in the library. I was particularly interested in including poems from times when conservation appeared to have been less of an urgent issue. I then wrote round to various modern poets asking them to send me any new poems to consider. When I had all the poems and the final choice had been agreed, I spent some time on the sequence of the poems. I wanted the anthology to tell a 'story' – but finish on a note of hope for the future ...

What kind of poems do you like reading?

Many kinds! Humorous, rhythmical, resonant, frightening, mysterious – especially the kind of poem that sends a shiver down your spine when it's heard, rather like certain pieces of haunting music might ... poems I wish I had written myself ...

Which of your own poems go down best with young people?

Humorous poems about things that they can relate to: a sister who annoys them ... a boy who interrupts ... wanting to open a present before it's your birthday. Poems about things which happen to all of us ... Poems which are about something rather mysterious and need a special, quiet atmosphere for reading ... back to the 'shiver down the spine' mentioned earlier.

What are the important decisions which need to be taken when you are putting together an anthology?

Is every poem worth reading? ... Is each poem relevant to the overall theme in some way or other? Is there a good variety of poems in terms of subject, style, modern, old ...? Does the position of the poems work well? I enjoy placing poems together in a way which creates extra interest and sets off each poem well ...

How important is artwork in a poetry anthology?

I think it can be very valuable ... especially for young readers: a poem uses language in a very concentrated way and too many on a page can be rather like trying to swallow the starters, turkey and Christmas pudding all in one go!

How important is the title of an anthology?

The title is extremely important. It needs to attract people to the book in the first place ... Funnily enough, this particular title *What on Earth ...?* was there right from the beginning.

What advice would you give to a young anthologist?

First of all choose what you like: you'll want your anthology to reflect your own personal choice of poetry. However, after that, try to re-read 'in someone else's shoes' and check the variety ...

The aim here is to make your own poetry anthology for young people.

Which of the poems you have just been reading did you like most? Why was that?

Look at Judith Nicholls' answer about what kind of poetry she likes again. Which kinds do you like best?

Stage 1

Either working on your own or in a small group, decide whether your anthology is going to have a theme like *What on Earth. ...?* or whether you are going to organise it in some other way.

Stage 2

Read as many poems as you can possibly lay your hands on! Use what your English teachers can give you, the school library, your public library and anywhere else you can think of.

Stage 3

Make sure you have got a good variety of poems, including some of your own or your friends'. (You could use the poem you wrote on page 49.)

Stage 4

Try out your selection of poems on other people of your own age. Ask them if there are any poems which they think are not worth reading and if so why not.

Stage 5

Add photographs and artwork that you would like to go with your anthology.

Stage 6

Think of a good title for it.

Stage 7

Decide what order the poems should be in. Look at what Judith Nicholls says about this.

Stage 8

Design a front and back cover and 'publish' your anthology for the rest of your class.

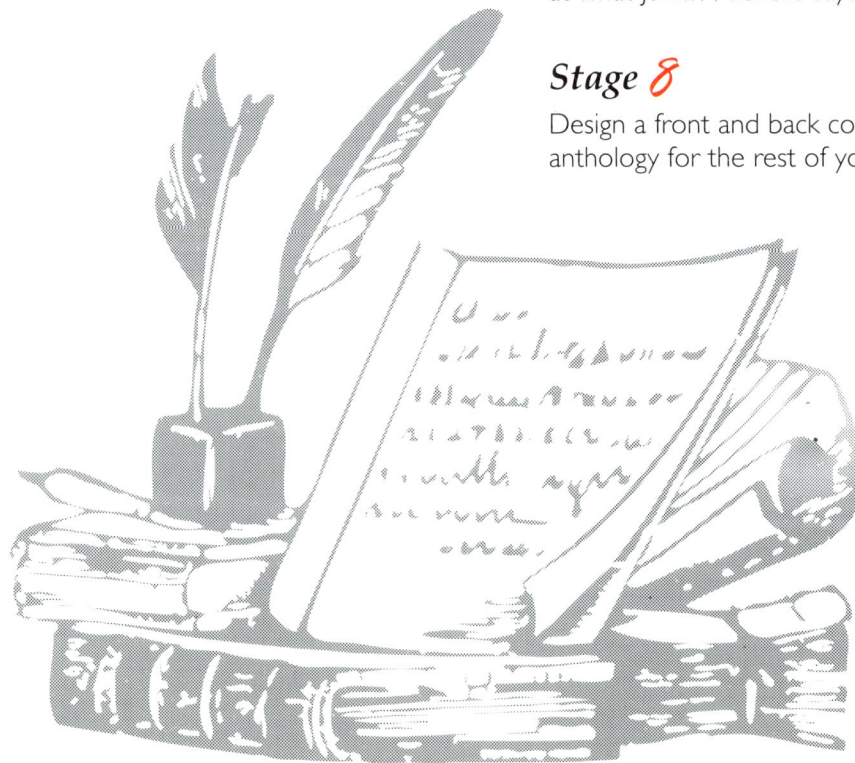

Other Things to Do with a Poem

On pages 50–55 you read a number of poems. Here are some things you might like to try out with them or with other poems you read.

◆ Simply enjoy a poem and think about what it is saying!

(Try this on *This is Just to Say* and *Raw Carrots*)

◆ Read a poem aloud, either on your own or in a group, and make a tape-recording of it.

(You could try this out with *The Song of the Homeworkers*)

◆ Write a poem in the same style as the poem you have read.

(For example, you could write your own animal poem like *The Moth* or *The Spider* in which you look very closely at a particular insect. You need to think what it reminds you of, what is unusual about it and what you think it does.

Or you could write a poem like Mike Rosen's. You would need to think of a situation at home, something that happens to all of us. It might be a situation in which you always end up arguing with your parents or guardians. You would need to think what you say in this kind of situation and include speech in your poem.)

◆ Make up five really good questions to ask someone about a poem to get them thinking about it.

◆ Write a letter to the writer of a poem. You could ask her or him questions about the poem and what it means. You could say what you thought and why you enjoyed it (if you did!)

◆ You could make a poster to go with a poem you have really enjoyed, perhaps including your favourite lines from the poem on your poster.

◆ You could play around with a poem using a wordprocessor. Type it into the memory and then delete certain words, leaving a line or a blank space where you have taken words out. Print out your version and give it to someone else in your class. See if they can guess what the missing words might be!

◆ You could make up the story behind a poem. Guess what has been going on before or what is happening just 'out of sight' of your poem. You could make up a story or a newspaper article or a short play – whatever grabs your imagination!

◆ You could make a video of your friends talking about their favourite poems. You might want to have particular music or sounds to go with them. Or you might want to read the poems in a special place.

Reflection

In this Unit you have been practising how to

● *ask and answer questions about poems*
● *take part in a group presentation*
● *express your own views about poems*
● *read poems aloud*
● *say which poems you prefer and why*
● *work out the meaning of a poem*
● *find and choose poems from a library*
● *read a range of poetry*
● *revise and draft poems*
● *write different kinds of poems*
● *assemble ideas on a wordprocessor*
● *use words in a deliberate order in a poem*

Talk to your friends and your teacher about the things you have been doing in this Unit. Decide how much you have understood and how much progress you have made. Filling in Unit 4 of the Record Sheet on page 84 will also help you think about what you have done in this Unit and the knowledge you are gaining in your English lessons.

This Unit gives you the opportunity to

- read a variety of letters and newspaper articles
- present information clearly
- read a brochure for information
- choose reference materials
- write for a variety of purposes

When you write a letter to a friend, you don't expect to see it printed out for everybody to read. When you write to a newspaper or a even a famous person you know that your letter may well be read by other people.

On these pages there are the following three types of letter.

1. Letters to the Editor of a young person's newspaper, *The Early Times*.

2. Letters to the Problem Page of the same newspaper.

3. Letters to Judy Blume the novelist, which she has put together into a book.

I In groups, read them aloud and quickly sort them into these three types.

Wrong ideas

I READ Jenna Jiggens' letter about teenagers bunking off.

Firstly, I would like to say that not all teenagers bunk off school, as Jenna implied.

Secondly, not all people who do bunk off school are teenagers. In fact some are of the same age as Jenna and younger.

Jenna has an idea that all teenagers are badly behaved and idiotic — is this the way she couple of years tim

I agree with h and that is that p school have got has it ever occ people are tryi about it?

Please Jenna on teenagers a who skip scho

Popping a question

WHEN I hear some of the pop n around these days, I can't help wor ing how some people listen to it.

However, this is not the thing bothers me — people are perfectly to listen to pop music if they wish, long as they don't force other people listen to it too.

I am one of the few people that ca stand pop music, but whenever I wa into a shop it's the first thing I hear. record shops, only a very small space given to classical music. Whenever a tapes or records are on special offer, it always pop music or jazz — hardly eve classical music.

I realise I'm in minority, and I don expect shops to play classical music a the time, or record shops to devote al their shelves to classical music, but I wonder how pop music fans would feel if the only thing they ever heard any-where was classical music?

Dear Judy,

I am twelve years old. I have a brother who is a month old and parents who take advantage of me. The main reason I am writing is I want your advice. Ever since my mom had the baby I don't have any privacy. They expect me to do everything (clean the house, take care of the cats, etc.) but since I just started seventh grade I have a lot of tests and home-work. They expect me to get my homework done in an hour so I can do my chores. Well, it's impossible.

I've tried explaining my side but they don't under-stand. I've told my friends and they don't know what I should do. Do you know what I should do? Please, I need your help. Another thing I meant to tell you was my parents also make fun of me. They say I have a bad personality or I'm getting chunky and other things that really hurt. I really would like your advice. Thanks!

Kimberly, age 12

Bad stutter

Dear Jo,

I have an awful problem. I have a very bad stutter. This means that when I read in class, I can't say half of the words. This is terribly embarrassing and it means I am now scared of reading.

Sometimes I get laughed at which is very upsetting. I have talked to my parents about it but they say it's because I don't get enough sleep or because I am excited about something.

Does this mean that every time I get tired or excited about some-thing I get this dreadful embarrassing stutter?

Please, please help me.

Dear Judy,

I am from Birmingham, England. My name is Jeanne Ann and I hate it. It sounds soppy and boring. I would much rather be called Harriet. That sounds dramatic and unusual. I like being unusual and daring. I would love to be very flamboyant and a bit eccentric. But my Mum and Dad don't know this side of me.

Jeanne Ann, age 14

g water costs

other day on the news I
people talking about the
n costs of water.

he following couple of
I heard people saying
it was awful because
es were going up. I think
is disgraceful because
ames Water need the money
build more sufficient filter
d cleaning equipment in
der that we receive clean
d hygienic water.

People don't realise what
hey are saying. They should
e grateful that they even have
water for some less fortunate
than us don't receive clean
drinkable water. I think we are
very lucky.

To save space, letters in a newspaper or magazine are normally set out without addresses being printed in full. They are also written in a range of styles: some use short sentences, some use more complicated ones to put over what the writer is trying to say.

1 Study the letters carefully. Pick out examples of short and longer sentences. Why do you think the writer has chosen to write in this way? What punctuation has been used?

2 Read this reply to the letter from the person with the stutter:

It sounds like your classroom stutter is a relatively new problem as you say mum and dad think it is caused by lack of sleep or excitement.

They may be right. Is there something else that is getting you worked up and interfering with your sleep? We are never at our best if we are tired and, of course, reading in front of the class makes most people feel at least a little excited or embarrassed. I'll bet lots of your classmates blush or fidget, stammer or sniff when it is their turn to read. Watch them closely and you'll notice their signs of embarrassment.

To help with your stutter, try reading out loud at home. Start in your own room with the door closed. Probably the main thing to remember is to try to speak slowly. Read favourite passages from favourite books or recite familiar poems. Try recording your practice sessions and listen for improvement as time goes on.

2 Which one of these letters did you find most interesting?

Have you ever written a letter like any of these?

Do you like reading other people's letters? If so, where do you normally read them?

In your groups answer these questions for each type of letter.

◆ What kind of topics are normally written about?

◆ Why do you think someone writes this kind of letter?

◆ What kind of reply would they expect? Would it be private or public?

3 Either continue this reply offering as much helpful advice as you can think of, or write a reply to one of these letters, suitable for publication in a newspaper for people of your own age.

Try and use more complicated sentences where you think it would make your ideas clearer.

Some local newspapers give schools in their area the opportunity to produce a number of pages about themselves.

All these articles were written by school students of about your age.

KEEP IT CLEAN

DO YOU CARE?

by Anne-Marie Crust & Amanda Adams

We can all help by making sure that pupils are properly educated about the environment and don't take it for granted.

If we do not take care of the environment now it will affect us in years to come.

Global warming will melt the ice caps in the North Pole and could flood the earth.

Joanne Howard, environmental health officer for Hounslow and her division deals with a range of matters which include noise problems and air pollution.

As Hounslow is near to Heathrow Airport there are a lot of problems with noise.

If you find this affects you, you can ring a special telephone number.

Our school is very concerned about the environment. On Friday, November 17 a group of girls in the third year collected litter from the boundaries of the school.

They collected six full bags of litter one of which was full of cans that are going towards the Blue Peter Appeal.

They are also collecting used paper which is going to be recycled.

A lot of us feel strongly about the state of our environment.

The hole in the ozone layer is getting bigger day by day and unless we stop using things like CFCs and carbon dioxide, we will all suffer from skin cancer.

We should be more aware of the earth's problems and take action. Already quite a lot of people use ozone friendly aerosols.

We carried out a survey in our school to see how many people took notice of environmental problems.

• 73 per cent of the school said they use unleaded petrol. Although some people couldn't change from using leaded to unleaded petrol because of mechanical problems.

• 78 per cent of the school said they use ozone friendly sprays, we weren't very surprised at this because of the publicity of ozone friendly sprays.

We felt pleased about the fact that the demand for furs had decreased, only 34 per cent of the school owned furs.

Not many people used recycled paper or tissue, although there was an increase in the amount of people who used waste paper bins—72 per cent of the school said they use these.

Only 17 per cent of the school took old bottles to their local bottle banks.

Lesley Azariah & Sami Shori

Vanessa's key to stardom

The Green School was the start of a brilliant musical career for pianist Vanessa Latarche from Isleworth. She has gained world-wide fame as a soloist, recitalist and chamber musician.

Vanessa started to pay the piano at ten which is unusual for a well established pianist. Remarkably within three years, at the age of 13, she passed eight grades, sending her well on her way to fame and fortune.

She started to attend the Green School in 1970 and was a member of Oaks House. During her time at the Green School, she attended private lessons. After leaving school she continued to study the piano at The Royal College of Music, where she now teaches.

Vanessa has fond memories of her time at the school. In particular the productions she took part in with Isleworth Grammar School, now Isleworth and Syon School.

She told us that she used to play while the pupils came into assembly. This is still a tradition in the school.

Her memories include one in which she had a wonderful excuse for missing PE lessons. It was necessary for her to take special care of her hands. Instead she used this time to practice.

She is still very conscious of what she does with her hands. They are not insured, although she feels they should be.

As many famous artists, Vanessa has had her share of embarrassing moments. She has had pedals fall off and notes stick at major concerts.

At the moment Vanessa is giving a recital in Japan. In December she will play for the Queen at St. James' Palace, London.

KATHERINE VAUGHAN & RENIE PAUL

...HOOL THE ...OMBS DID ...OT STOP

It started next to public house

...at the Green School ... lucky escape in ...ber 1940! The ...was bombed by the ...s!

...damage was ...e. Had the bombs ...ring term time the ...would have been ...ing.

...t takes more than a ...bs to get rid of the ...hool! This did not ... end to lessons ...aching carried on ...d school in St. ...ad.

...chool began as a ...chool next to the ...ondon Apprentice ...eworth in 1796. It ...turned into a day

school for primary children and finally a Secondary School for Girls.

The school was bursting at its seams as more pupils joined the force! To ease the squash, girls moved to another disused school in St. Johns Road, but only until new buildings were built.

Finally, a bigger and better building was found for the girls at Busch Corner. At last a home was found and they could settle down!

As a result of the

bombing during the war new buildings were again needed! In 1977 the building of the new block brought more opportunities.

Unfortunately it was built on top of the best tennis courts. But the girls preferred the modernisations it brought with it! Science laboratories, languages, domestic science and art rooms were included.

Laura McLennan & Sarah Jeremiah

1 What impression do you receive of The Green School from these three articles?

What do you know about the history of your own school? Does your school have any famous ex-students? Who? What are the issues that are important to you and your friends? Is the environment one of them?

2 Working in groups, write three articles suitable for publication in a local newspaper about your own school.

Starting Writing

Decide on what image you would like to put across about your school and who you think might be reading your articles.

Organise any necessary research. For example you might want to do some of these things.

◆ use your school's library

◆ talk to teachers or other staff who have worked at the school for a long time

◆ interview the headteacher about what she or he thinks is important for the school now or about anything else you want to know

◆ conduct a survey among other students about an issue that you think is important

◆ invite someone important in your local area to be interviewed

◆ cover a sports or arts event at school

Or you can do anything else that appeals to you!

Decide who is going to produce each article.

Composing

If possible, use a wordprocessor to do a first draft of your articles and print them out.

Revising

Show your articles to the others in your group. Get their comments and make any necessary changes.

Check your spelling and presentation. Use a spell-checker or dictionary.

Publishing

Produce a final and neat draft of your articles. If possible, use the 'end-justify' function to produce columns of print. Cut and paste these into a class newspaper feature on your school.

You could approach the editor of your local newspaper and see if she or he would consider doing a feature on your school along the lines of the material you have produced.

Not everything in a newspaper is news. An article might be written about something that happened some time ago.

Read this article from *The Indy*, a weekly newspaper for young people published by *The Independent* newspaper.

6 FEATURES

They were only obeying orders

Do you always do what you are told? This famous test suggest that ordinary people will do practically anything

How OBEDIENT are you? If you were instructed to give a massive electric shock to an innocent stranger strapped into a chair, would you obey and turn on the current? No? Research by psychologist Stanley Milgram suggests otherwise.

In Milgram's studies, ordinary people were recruited through newspaper advertisements to help with an experimental study. They were told it was 'an investigation into the effects of punishment on learning'. In each study there was a 'teacher' and a 'learner'.

The learner was strapped into a chair. Electrodes were placed on his wrists. He was told to learn a list of word pairs. Whenever he made a mistake he was punished by the teacher with an electric shock.

In fact, the real focus of the

The man in the electric chair is an actor. He is not connected to the power. The real subject of the experiment is the ordinary

study was on the teacher. He sat in the next room in front of an imposing shock generator. The generator had thirty

The average shock his teachers were prepared to administer was 375 volts

switches which were marked from 15 volts to 450 volts and labelled with descritpions ranging from 'Slight Shock' to 'Danger: Severe Shock'.

The teacher was told that every time the learner made a mistake, he must be given a shock; a small shock for the first mistake, increasing in voltage for every subsequent error.

In reality the learner was

person with his finger on the power switches – will he electrocute the actor just because he is told to by the authority

an actor, and did not actually receive any shocks. By prior arrangement the learner deliberately made lots of mistakes. The objective: to see how far the teacher would go. Would he stop after giving a relatively small shock, or would he go on to give a shock of three or four hundred volts?

The teacher's dilemma began as soon as the learner indicated discomfort. At 75 volts he grunted; at 120 volts he made a verbal complaint; at 150 volts he demanded to leave the experiment. His demands to be set free became more and more distressed and emotional. At 285 volts he gave an agonized yell.

figure? The answer is yes. Most people (66 per cent) will turn the power up beyond the point where the actor begs them to stop.

If at any time a teacher refused to give a shock, he was simply ordered to continue. Only when a teacher complete-

Two-thirds of the teachers carried on all the way to 450 volts

ly refused to go on was the experiment concluded.

Much to his surprise, Milgram found that the average shock his teachers were prepared to administer was 375 volts. Two-thirds of them carried on all the way to 450 volts. Some of the teachers showed only minor signs of tension throughout the experiment. Others were very

agitated: they trembled and sweated, and after the final shock they mopped their brows and nervously fumbled for cigarettes.

Were the teachers different from ordinary people? Were they torturers and sadists?

Not at all: Milgram's subjects were orinary people, selected from a deliberately wide variety of social and professional backgrounds. It seems that in certain situations, most people will obey instructions to carry out immoral acts; and that probably includes YOU.

The most worrying aspect of Milgram's work is its implications for society. It suggests that we are all far more willing than we imagine to engage in unthinkable acts of aggression and cruelty. This is born out by real events. In the 1930's and 1940's millions of Jews were gassed to death by German soldiers. After the war, the same soldiers explained that they were only obeying orders.

More recently, American soldiers slaughtered every man, woman and child in the Vietnamese village of My Lai. They offered the same explanation as the Germans.

The reason for writing an article like this is that it is interesting. It doesn't matter whether it is something that has just happened or not. This kind of article is called a **feature.**

2 Look up the meanings of these difficult words and any others that you do not understand :

psychologist, recruited, imposing, subsequent, prior, objective, dilemma, verbal, concluded, subjects, implications.

Check that your definition of a word 'works' by trying it in the passage you have just read.

3 What did the people who took part think that the point of the experiment was?

What was Milgram trying to show in his experiment?

What point does his experiment make to you? Does it surprise you? How do you think you would have behaved in this situation?

Do you always do as you are told?

4 Write a feature on something that happened in the past but is still of interest to young people now, suitable for publication in a young persons' newspa

Starting Writing

Research your topic. You will need to discuss with your teacher or librarian the best way of getting at the kind of information you require.

Composing

Make a first draft of your article, if possible using a wordprocessor.

Revising

Read your first draft to someone. Ask them for their comments and make any necessary changes.

Proof-reading

Check your spelling and punctuation. Use a dictionary.

Decide how you are going to publish your feature. Produce your final and neat draft.

Reviewing Books for Newspapers

Often you will find short reviews of books in newspapers.

Both these reviews were written by young people of your own age.

by Ailyn Routledge, 13, from Cumbria

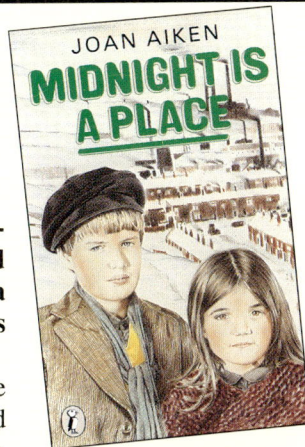

This book is set in the middle of the 19th century, and the main character is a young orphan named Lucas Bell.

Lucas is bored with the monotony of his life and wants a friend desperately. Then one day a young French girl comes to live in Midnight Court, the rambling home of his disagreeable guardian Sir Randolph. Some unexpected things happen which drastically change his life.

I strongly recommend **Midnight is a Place** to anyone over 11 years old who enjoys reading for pleasure.

It has a good plot which is very exciting, but it is also a bit gruesome in places.

This book is educational, because it taught me a bit about life as a working class person in the mid-19th century.

● **Midnight is a Place by Joan Aiken, published by Puffin**

by Stephen Chambers, 12, from Leeds

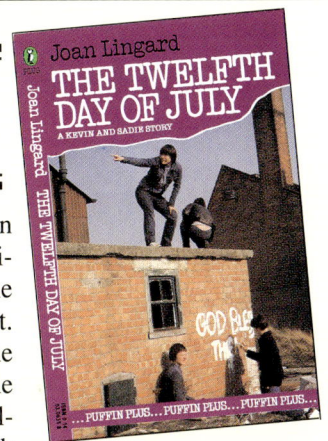

This extremely well-written book is about two Irish families living in Belfast, one Catholic and one Protestant. The Catholics loathe the Protestants and vice versa; the story is mainly about the children having fights with each other and painting slogans on walls that were offensive to the other religion.

Although it is fiction, **The Twelfth Day of July** is based on fact. The story depicts life in a few cities in Northern Ireland today. The Protestants and Catholics don't get on and the arguments the children on both sides have are similar. While I was reading the book I thought these disputes were pointless and wondered why Catholics and Protestants couldn't get on with each other, even if they did have different ideas.

The Twelfth Day of July is written by Joan Lingard and published by Puffin. I recommend the book for ages 10-15.

1 In groups, talk about these reviews. Do you know either of these books? If so, do you agree with what these two reviewers have said?

What is the point of a book review?

What are the important things to include in a book review? Make a list of these.

What should you not include in a book review?

2 Write a book review of your own for a book you have recently read and enjoyed.

Start a class selection of book reviews which you can add to whenever you have read a book.

What's in a Holiday?

1 What kind of holiday do you enjoy? What is the best holiday that you can remember?

What kind of things do you like to avoid when you are on holiday?

What is the worst thing that you can remember happening to you when you were on holiday? What is the most amusing thing that has ever happened to you on a holiday?

2 Look at and read the details in these pages from holiday brochures.

B

MAJORCA
Calas de Mallorca

GORDON T GOPHER KIDS CLUB See the pages 6...

Hotel & Apartments Aguamar Club
CALAS DE MALLORCA

'Attractive pool area and excellent indoor and outdoor activities. Very suitable for families. In a quieter part of the resort.'

Previously known as the Aubamar Club, this is one of Majorca's most up-to-date holiday developments. It is a complex of hotel and apartment buildings on high ground about 400 metres from the resort centre and about 1.5 kms from the beach. However, on-the-spot amenities are comprehensive enough to provide all your holiday pleasures with no need to go elsewhere.

● Large swimming pool comprising three sections; furnished terraced area with palms; sunbeds for hire. ● Three bars and pool bar. ● Apartments guests have full use of restaurant with self-service from buffets. ● Barbecue area open lunchtime and evening. ● Full and varied entertainments programme: watersports games during day; cabaret parties. ● Two tennis-courts, hourly charge. ● Children's playground, play area with sand; nursery; highchairs and cots free. ● Maid service in apartments three times a week.

Hotel rooms with two or three beds (or four bedded rooms with bunk beds), private bath, shower, toilet and balcony. **Half board.** Child prices: age limit 12. Reductions for 3rd & 4th adult are in the Price List.

Official rating: 3 stars.

Studio (1-3 persons): living room with twin beds or a bed-settee, kitchenette with cooking facilities, fridge, bathroom and a balcony or terrace. **1 bedroom apartment (2-5 persons):** as studios with separate twin bedroom and three sofa-beds in living room.

self-catering

Child prices: age limit 16.

Official rating: 3 keys.

More for your money

1st child pays 1st child price for departures 1 Jun & 16 Sep-21 Oct.
...es only in hotel rooms

The Aq...

...Complex

One of the ap...

A

Showtime

9-12 & 13-15 years
DRAMA + MULTI-ACTIVITY

This could be your big break ... a chance to put on a show and get to grips with the skills and techniques of drama and stagecraft.

Spend half of each day with our experienced drama instructors at the Camp Theatre, and the rest of your time on the Freetime multi-activity programme.

No particular experience is required, just plenty of energy and enthusiasm. Our instructors will introduce you to a broad range of performance and technical support skills throughout the week:

Acting	Voice Projection
Script-Writing	Set Design
Miming	Costume Design
Dancing	Make-up

Video playbacks are also used during rehearsals to give showtimers a sneak preview of their individual performances.

Showtimers apply these skills to their preferred role in the special end-of-week production. Everyone gets a spot in the limelight and the entire show is performed before a full audience of other freetimers.

At each Camp there are excellent venues for the Showtime courses:
Claremont: Joyce Grenfell Theatre
Charterhouse: Ben Travers Theatre
Southdowns: Lupton Hall

PRICE PER WEEK: £119

Available at all camps
Please refer to page 18 for details on dates available at each camp

WHERE ARE YOU GOING FOR YOUR HOLIDAY THIS YEAR?

NOWHERE SPECIAL. JUST THAT ACTIVITY HOLIDAY IN A SPANISH LUXURY HOTEL

SOUNDS PRETTY BORING TO ME

C 11

MULTI-ACTIVITY HOLIDAYS

Mini-Breaks

PGL Adventure Weekends
For 8-11's, 10-13's and 12-16's

Unlike most other children's holiday companies, PGL own many of the centres featured in this brochure and organise adventure holidays almost year round, from the end of February right through until October.

At all times of year our centres are staffed and equipped to the same high standards you expect of PGL during the summer and, consequently, we are able to offer children exciting adventure weekends in the spring, early summer and autumn.

PGL Adventure Weekends run from Friday evening through until Sunday evening and, as with all other PGL holidays, almost everything is included. There is a fixed programme selected from the centre's activities and the weekend will be packed with fun from the moment your child arrives.

Adventure Weekends are organised at Boreatton Park, Thornley Hall, Dalguise and also at centres in the Wye Valley and Brecon Beacons. In the case of the latter two areas, we shall advise you of the actual centre with your final information details, approximately 2 weeks before the holiday. Within each area, all the centres are close together and

accommodation is of a similar standard.

To help make the most of the time available for an Adventure Weekend, it would be most convenient if parents could deliver and collect their children, but we can arrange to pick up from the station nearest to the centre if required — see pages 48 & 49 for details and prices. Please note: our only collection service is at 7 p.m. on Fridays, with return back to the station for 6 p.m. on Sundays.

ACTIVITY TASTERS
For 8-11's and 10-13's

If you would like your child to enjoy a PGL multi-activity holiday during the summer, without being away from home for a full week, then a PGL Activity Taster during August is the answer. These mini-breaks take place at Boreatton Park, giving a three or four night stay at the centre. PGL Tasters have an allocation of exciting activities from the full week programme and, of course, the normal, friendly attention of our excellent centre staff. They are ideal for first-timers and give a good opportunity to see what PGL is all about. Please note that escorted travel is only available on Saturdays, so you can bring or collect them and let them take PGL travel in the other direction. Single fares are available in conjunction with Activity Tasters.

Booking DETAILS

DATES	HOLIDAY CODES	PRICE inc. VAT
4- 7 August	AT1	£99
7-11 August	AT2	£124
11-14 August	AT3	£93
14-18 August	AT4	£118
18-21 August	AT5	£87
21-25 August	AT6	£112
25-28 August	AT7	£81
28 Aug-1 Sept	AT8	£106

Booking DETAILS

Centres/Areas:	Boreatton Park	Wye Valley	Brecon Beacons	Thornley Hall	Dalguise
Location	Shropshire Borders	Near Ross-on-Wye	Near Brecon	Near Oxford	Scotland
Age Range	8-11, 10-13	8-11, 10-13 or 12-16	8-11, 10-13 or 12-16	8-11, 10-13	8-11, 10-13 or 12-16
Accommodation Type	Indoor or Leisure Homes	Indoor	Indoor or Leisure Homes	Indoor	Indoor or Leisure Homes
Available Weekends commencing Fridays between	16/3 - 29/6 14/9	23/3 - 22/6	23/3 - 22/6 14/9 - 5/10	16/3 - 6/7	13/4 - 8/6 7/9 - 28/9
Centre featured on page	12 & 13	19 & 20	16 & 17	21	25
HOLIDAY CODE	WE50	WE53	WE5	WE54	WE59
PRICE PER WEEKEND inc. VAT	£65	£65	£65	£65	£65

Insurance for Weekends & Tasters costs £8. A deposit of £25 is payable at the time of booking, or the full sum if within 12 weeks of the holiday commencing.

PGL ADVENTURE
0989 768 768

D

👑 👑 👑
APARTHOTEL RIOMAR

FACILITIES	●●●
CHILDREN	●●
ENTERTAINMENT	●●

In our opinion . . . These apartments are quietly situated, yet within easy reach of Alcudia. Families will find them particularly appealing.

In the quieter part of the Bay of Alcudia, the Aparthotel Riomar opened just two years ago. The floors have been arranged in a series of tiers to give every balcony a sunny aspect. Other striking features include the swimming pool set among terraces and gardens, a comfortable lounge for evening entertainment and facilities for tennis and squash. The marvellous beach of soft white sand is just a couple of minutes' stroll across the main road and you'll find shops, bars and restaurants within 800 yards. If you feel like exploring further afield, there are regular buses into the port of Alcudia (three miles away) and to nearby C'an Picafort as well.

APARTHOTEL AMENITIES INCLUDE

● Pool, sun terrace and garden; bar service to pool.
● Bar opening onto terrace; lounge.
● Restaurant with a la carte menu.
● Tennis, table tennis.
● Resident entertainer.
● Children's section of pool; cots; high chairs.

ACCOMMODATION

There are two sizes of apartment. **Studios** (for 2/4 persons) have twin beds, plus a convertible sofa-bed when required. **One-bedroomed apartment** (for 2/4 persons) have a twin-bedded room, plus two sofa-beds in the lounge. Both types have a kitchenette, bathroom and balcony. Maid service is provided.

SPECIAL OFFER

Two weeks for the price of one on selected dates in May and October (see Price & Flight Guide for details).

Self catering.
A complimentary food pack will be in your apartment on arrival.
No. of apartments: 120

The children's paddling pool

Child Reductions
All children up to 16 years qualify for child reductions at the Riomar.

Riomar is great for children

PRICES & FLIGHTS
See the separate Horizon Summer Sun Price & Flight Guide for full details.

HORIZON

29

What's in a Holiday?

2 Study this chart. Which of the four holidays would suit these people? Copy and complete it.

	Holiday A Showtime	Holiday B Calas de Mallorca	Holiday C PGL Weekend	Holiday D Aparthotel Riomar
Enjoys tennis	✘	✔	?	✔
Enjoys sunshine				
Enjoys designing clothes				
Enjoys outside activities				
Enjoys swimming				
Prefers to be away from adults				
Prefers to be with adults				
Likes evening activities				
Likes good food				
Likes going on excursions				

Key: *?* – not sure
           ✔ – definitely
           ✘ – unlikely to be suitable

What other types of activities do you think there are? Which of these activities would suit you most?

What Makes a Good Holiday?

1   In pairs or small groups, find out what people of your own age think makes a good holiday by asking them.

Stage 1

Make up a list of questions to find out what each person in your class or year thinks is important in a holiday. Use the ideas you have been working on so far to help you think up questions.

Stage 2

Put your questions in order. You could use a wordprocessor to do this. Print or write out your final version as a questionnaire.

Stage 3

Try it out on your friends.

Stage 4

Use the information you have gathered to draw up a list of the essential ingredients of a good holiday. You may know how to use a computer to help you in this and possibly to print out your findings in a chart.

2   Using the ideas you have gained from the above activity, design four pages for a holiday brochure aimed particularly at people of your own age.

Stage 1

Research into the range of holidays currently on offer by getting some brochures from travel agents.

Stage 2

Select the four types of holiday you think would appeal to most of the people you have surveyed. Decide where they will be based. Don't forget to have a variety of costs to suit all purses!

Stage 3

Study the ways holidays are presented in the examples you have been working with. For example

◆   Remember that brochures are trying to sell holidays and therefore they try to make the holidays sound as interesting as possible.

◆   Look at the ways they use headings.

◆   Look at the way they use photographs.

◆   Look at the way information is divided up into short lists often with 'blobs' to indicate the major points.

Stage 4

Design and write your brochure as a first draft. Cut it out and paste it onto a page, including pictures or photographs if possible. Revise and proof-read your pages. If you want any help in drafting, look back at the model on page 49 in Unit 4.

Stage 5

Produce a final draft of your pages and brochure. Make and design a cover. Think of a snappy name for your young people's travel company!

Compare your brochure to the others in the class. Why are some more effective and more interesting than others? In particular, look at the writing, design and use of pictures.

Reflection

In this Unit you have been practising how to

● *respond positively to other people's ideas*
● *show you can understand the meaning of letters and newspaper articles*
● *select reference materials for a newspaper article*
● *express your own views on what you have read*
● *show how a writer's choice of words affects their message*
● *write a letter to a newspaper*
● *write a newspaper article*
● *write a book review for a newspaper*
● *plan and produce a holiday brochure*

Talk to your friends and your teacher about the things you have been doing in this Unit. Decide how much you have understood and how much progress you have made. Filling in Unit 5 of the Record Sheet on page 84 will also help you think about what you have done in this Unit and the knowledge you are gaining in your English lessons.

This Unit gives you the opportunity to

● *take part in role play*
● *understand how 'time' can be used in a story*
● *understand how stories can be structured*
● *read a story by a young writer*
● *write a story*

One of the exciting things about reading and writing stories is that you can jump about in time.

In this passage the writer uses a trick that can be particularly effective. A character goes into a garden and finds herself in another time.

Moondial

Her gaze travelled right to the furthest corner. There was a door, slightly ajar. Minty approached. Cautiously she pushed it open. There was another door beyond, also open. She passed between the cold stone-smelling walls and gave that a push, too.

'The garden!'

It lay quiet and faultless under the early sun. There were lawns, straight paths, yews and statues. Minty stepped on to the terrace and felt a thrill of recognition. She had never been here before, she knew, and yet had a strange knowledge that she was now stepping exactly where she was *meant* to step. This garden had been waiting for her.

Slowly she walked along the terrace. She paused to look up at the statues, as if expecting a sign on their stone faces. But they gave none. They gazed as they had always gazed, untouchable, intact. One was carrying stone fruit and flowers, the next was a lady with a flightless bird – a dove, perhaps. Now she went down the seven wide steps to the path that led to the centre of the garden.

No sooner had she done so than she became aware of being watched. She turned. No one was there. She lifted her eyes to the house itself. The windows were blank. She walked on, alert now, expectant. She had a curious sense of being drawn, of having no choice. As she went she was taking steps that had already been measured for her. She lifted her eyes and saw ahead, at the crossroads of the garden, another statue, and felt a prickling of

her shoulderblades. There was a power in the air, so strong that she could hardly breathe.

Minty stopped in front of the statue, with icy tides washing her from head to foot. There were an old man and a young boy, both winged like angels, though she was certain that they were not. They seemed to be wrestling, struggling for possession of a bowl above their heads and, catching a glimpse of a metal beak, Minty suddenly realized what it was.

'A sundial!' she exclaimed softly, and then, almost immediately and without knowing why – 'Moondial!'

And as she spoke the word a cold distinct wind rushed past her and the whole garden stirred and her ears were filled with a thousand urgent voices. She stood swaying. She put her hands over her ears and shut her eyes tight.

The whispers faded, the wind died. Minty opened her eyes and was blinded for a moment by the sun. But when she did see, she knew that she was in a now altered morning, not at all the morning she had woken up to.

Slowly she wheeled about. It seemed to her that under the changed sky the very garden had shrunk. She lifted her eyes to the house itself and saw smoke rising.

'There was none,' thought Minty. 'Not when I last looked!' and started to run back the way she had come.

She had reached the little stone passage that led to the courtyard when she met the boy – bumped into him, almost.

'Oh!' she gasped. 'Sorry!'

The boy, too, jumped back. He stood staring at her so pop-eyed, jaw dropped, that she

The character here is called Minty. Her mother is critically ill in hospital. She has gone to stay with her mother's friend who lives opposite a large stately home. As soon as Minty enters the garden she knows something odd is going to happen.

almost laughed.

'Oh my aunt! Oh my!' He was backing away, eyes enormous in his thin white face.

'What's the matter? Are you all right?' Minty said, while part of her mind had already taken in his dress, the rough jacket and queer woollen trousers, and knew that what she was seeing was what most people called a ghost.

'Oh ... oh!' he quavered. 'I ain't never seen one that *talked* before!'

'Who *are* you?' demanded Minty, affronted by this remark even though she did not understand it.

'I'll shut my eyes,' he said to himself. 'Then, when I open 'em – she'll have gone!'

'What cheek!' said Minty. '*I* will, then!'

She did so, though she did not in the least wish the boy to vanish. When she opened her eyes again it was just in time to see him cautiously unscrewing his own. They stared for a moment, then burst out laughing.

'Don't look as if we are going to disappear,' he said. 'Neither one of us.'

'No,' agreed Minty.

'Seen ghosts before, you know,' he continued. 'Well, bits and bobs of things, anyhow. But in broad daylight – and plain as the nose on your face!'

'Nor me,' said Minty. 'Here – what do you mean, ghost? *You're* the ghost!'

He laughed.

'Oh *yes,*' he said. 'I'm a ghost all right. That's why Cook told me to just run out for some raspberries for the pie. Run here, run there – wish I *was* a blessed ghost, and that's a fact!'

'I,' Minty told him coldly, 'have just come over from my Aunt Mary's house, and I don't think I imagined that!'

'Look,' he said, 'you could've just hopped out a rabbit-hole, for all I care.' He surveyed her narrowly. 'You're a bit of a let-down, for a ghost. I must be out of my head standing here rattling to you. I'd best be off and fetch them raspberries, if I don't want a whacking.'

'No! Wait! I've got an idea!'

'What?' His pinched white face was all at once alert, suspicious.

'Let's – let's shake hands!'

'Why?'

'Don't you see? Whichever of us is a ghost won't be able to, not properly. Ghosts go through things, they're not solid.'

He put out his hand and started down at it, and shook his head dubiously.

'Don't like the idea of it. Ugh! My hand going straight through yours! Ugh! Fair makes you shudder!'

'It won't.' Minty told him. 'It'll be the other way round. If *I* dare do it, why can't you?'

He looked at her.

'You're a girl, aren't you?' he said. 'Dressed in boy's clothes.'

She nodded.

'Blessed if I'll be beat by a girl,' he said. 'Here, then!'

He thrust out his hand, his face screwed in a grimace as if expecting to rouch something cold and slimy, and Minty put out hers. Their hands met and clasped. Warm solid flesh met warm solid flesh. The pair of them stood, hands locked, looking into one another's face in wonder.

'"We're both real!' said Minty softly at last. Then, 'What's your name?'

'Tom,' he said. 'Short for Edward.'

She laughed delightedly.

'I'm Minty. Short for Penelope.'

They were still holding hands.

'You a downstairs too, then?' he asked. 'What are you? Laundry? Scullery?'

'What are you?' she countered.

He shrugged. His face clouded and he pulled away his hand.

'All sorts. They've not decided. I'm up from the London house. Footman's what I'm after.'

'Footman?'

'I ain't big yet,' he said, 'but I shall be. Country air. Keep taking big snuffs of it, and I'll be six foot before Pinch knows!'

He took a big, sniffing breath, as if expecting to add half an inch to his height then and there. Instead, he fell into a bout of coughing. He bent double. His coughs were dry and racked.

'I suppose it must work the other way round,' Minty observed. 'I used to hold my breath to stop myself growing.'

Tom short for Edward straightened, gasping for breath.

'*Stop* yourself?' he said. 'Whatever –? Oh. You're a girl. Forgot. You'd never be a footman if you grew to seven foot, let alone six.'

'How old are you?' asked Minty.

He shrugged.

'Twelve abouts, I s'pose.'

'Don't you know?'

He shrugged again.

'Near enough, I do.'

'You've only got to ask your *mother*,' Minty told him.

'Dead.'

'Oh!' She was aghast. 'I'm sorry! I didn't–'

'And my pa.'

Minty stared. Suddenly she wanted to run away. She was looking at an orphan, and the very word orphan was terrible to her. It was a word that had been hovering perilously on the darkest edges of her own thoughts, a word she had tried to beat off as if it were a great black bat.

'An orphan,' he said.

Now the word was out, too late for her to clap her hands over her ears.

'Got brothers and sisters, though.'

Here was a straw, and Minty clutched it.

'Oh, that's good!' she cried with an enthusiasm that sounded ridiculous even to her own ears. 'I wish I had!' – this, at least, was genuine.

'Not that it matters a deal,' he went on, 'seeing I never see 'em!'

Calamity after calamity.

'Oh – but why not?'

'I'm here, see,' he told her patiently. 'They're there -- in London. Two of 'em's dead, anyhow.'

Minty stared at him. She simply could not take in all this death so casually spelt out. In her world, grandparents sometimes died, or perhaps a neighbour, hardly known so never missed. She was the only person of her age she knew whose father had died. She remembered how this had marked her out at the time. People had seemed to tiptoe round her, leaving careful space between them and her. She had seemed to stand alone in an invisible circle.

This boy stood in acres of loneliness.

'Don't you miss them?' It was all she could think of to say.

'Bit.' Then, after a pause. 'Miss our Dorrie, a bit. Funny nugget, she is. Makes me laugh.'

'How old is she?'

'Seven or eight abouts. Tried to keep her with me. I did, but they said she was too little. Would've liked her with me.'

His thin white face pulled long and sad. Minty could think of nothing to say.

'Still 'n all, once I'm six foot and a footman I'll have her here, all right!'

He took in several snuffing breaths as if to hurry this moment forward but he ended by coughing again, dreadfully.

'Needs some antibiotics,' thought Minty, wisely, and was about to say as much when a shout came from behind her.

'Here – you – whatsyername – boy!'

Tom straightened, eyes still watering, and Minty turned. A man stood there, leather-aproned and gartered, a gardener, she guessed.

'You coming for them raspberries or ain't yer? Birds've had hours at 'em already!'

'I'm – I'm coming now, sir!'

'You come here. Come on.'

Tom went and Minty watched. The boy looked skinnier and smaller than ever standing before the great burly man.

'New from London, ain't you?'

Tom nodded.

'Yes, sir.'

It was as if he were trying to make himself smaller now.

'Ain't heard of dawn, in London, I daresay. Or birds.'

Tom was silent.

Then the big man began to speak in a voice surprisingly soft and to punctuate his words with swift cuffs on Tom's head.

'*Birds* get up at *dawn*, whatsyername. Birds go peck, peck, peck –' (three swift cuffs, using both hands) and they go –'

'Oh, don't!' cried Minty, but she might never have spoken for all the notice he took. 'It's my fault he's late – he was talking to me!'

'*Boys* from *London*,' went on the terrible gardener, 'wants *learning* what's *what*!'

Tom had his hands up to his head now, to protect himself.

Minty ran to him.

'Stop it!' she cried. 'Please!'

But the soft voice and the cuffs went on, she might as well not have existed.

'*Stop* it!' she screamed and with her fists started to pummel the man and –

'Oh!' She gasped to find herself standing and aiming punches at the empty air. 'Oh!'

She let her hands fall, and as she did so had a swift, unmistakable memory of the feel of leather. She spread out her hands and looked at them, and they too seemed to be sending a message to say that they had, if only for a fraction of a second, beaten like birds against that vanished man, and could still remember the feel of that cold leather.

Helen Cresswell

A story like this needs a special kind of writing. If the reader is going to believe that someone has gone forwards or backwards in time, they have to be prepared first. Helen Cresswell does this by carefully building up atmosphere before the important moment when Minty discovers the moondial, her key into another time.

1 In small groups, look at the first five paragraphs again in detail. How did you feel as you read them? What did you think they were leading up to?

There are five senses. How many of them does Helen Cresswell appeal to in these paragraphs? Find as many examples as you can. Use this chart to help you.

Sense	Example
Smell	She passed between cold stone smelling walls.

People often talk about a sixth sense. What do you think they mean by this? Do you believe that some people do have a sixth sense? Do you, yourself?

Helen Cresswell seems to want us to believe that Minty has a sixth sense. What examples of this can you find? Add them to your chart.

Re-read the rest of the story. In what ways do you think Tom and Minty are alike? In what ways are they different?

2 Look at these quotations from *Moondial*. Decide where they come.

'Needs some antibiotics,' thought Minty ...

'You a downstairs too, then?' he asked. 'What are you? Laundry? Scullery?'

'You're a girl aren't you?' he said, 'Dressed in boy's clothes.'

'That's why cook told me to just run out for some raspberries for the pie.'

Minty stared at him. She simply could not take in all this death so casually spelt out. In her world, grandparents sometimes died or perhaps a neighbour, hardly known so never missed. She was the only person of her age she knew whose father had died.

Decide what each one tells you about the two different times that the characters live in.

3 When do you think Tom was alive? What is there in the story to help you decide?

Do some research in your school library into what it was like to be a servant. See if you can discover the different jobs that servants did, how much money they were paid, what age they started working as servants, what they wore and how much free time they had.

Study these pictures. Find out what each one tells you about the life of a servant.

What do you think Tom's life was like?

4 In pairs, imagine that one of you is Tom and one of you is his little sister Dorrie. Have a conversation in which Tom talks about his meeting with the stranger in the garden.

Stage 1

Look back at the passage to find out how old Dorrie is.

Stage 2

Decide how Tom has managed to get time off to meet her.

Stage 3

Decide where they are meeting. In London? Or in the country?

Stage 4

Improvise your conversation.

5 At the end of the passage you have been reading, Minty returns to her own time. What do you think she would be thinking and feeling?

Do you think she would want to tell anyone about what happened to her? Why might she want to tell someone? Why might she prefer to keep this experience a secret?

In the book Minty makes a tape to play to her mother who is in hospital in a coma. She hopes the tape might be unusual enough to bring her mother out of the coma. In it she describes everything that has been happening to her including her journeys in time.

Imagine that you are Minty making the first part of the tape in which you describe your meeting with Tom.

Read Moondial *for yourself to find out what happens in the rest of the story.*

Helen Cresswell based the story of *Moondial* on a real house that had been standing for several hundred years. Authors who write time-slip stories, where characters find themselves in a different time, often find it helpful to set their stories in a place with an interesting history. Sometimes they even use real historical details.

This time-slip story was written by three people of your own age. Each one decided to tell a part of the whole story. The asterisks show where one writer stops and the next begins. Before they started they were given this information about their local history.

The Last of Ernie Toffet

As Anita collected her books together for her daily lessons, she remembered the strange noises she had heard the previous night.

'I'll have to tell someone!' she thought.

Anita knew her parents would never believe her and anyway they were busy preparing for her father's business trip. Yes, she would have to tell Ms Godfrey.

Ms Godfrey was Anita's tutor. She was a tall woman with mousy coloured hair, which she always wore scraped back into a tight bun. Ms Godfrey could be strict at times but she never told Anita off unless it was for a good reason. Anita could trust Ms Godfrey, she could rely on her to be understanding.

Reluctantly Anita slowly walked to the study where her lessons were held. She remembered that they were going to do history for today's new topic and she had hardly prepared for it.

'Good morning!' Ms Godfrey greeted Anita cheerfully. She flashed Anita one of her amazing sparkling 100-watt smiles. Ms Godfrey had perfect teeth, each set in the exact correct position, and they were always gleaming white.

'Ms Godfrey ... ' began Anita.

'Yes, what is it?' replied Ms Godfrey in her smooth velvety voice.

'Last night I woke up when I heard a noise. At first I thought it was just the wind, but I decided to investigate.'

'Go on,' said Ms Godfrey encouragingly.

'Well, I thought it was coming from that cupboard – you know the one, at the bottom of the landing. I didn't see anyone, but the window was wide open and I know that you always go round and shut all the windows every night.'

'Have you any idea who might have opened it?' asked Ms Godfrey.

Anita could tell Ms Godfrey didn't really believe her, but she felt she was just politely listening.

That night Anita decided to stay awake and watch out. At about midnight she heard the sound of a window opening yet again. Cautiously she tiptoed down the chilly landing. The only light was the light of the street lamp shining through the window.

Silently she turned the knob on the door of the cupboard. Using all the courage she had in her, she thrust the door open, half expecting to see a strange alien being standing there. Instead she saw a young boy of about thirteen years looking around himself wonderingly.

*

Ernie Toffet was a rascally little lad. He was just under thirteen, but many mistook him for a ten year old he was so small. He had trouble seeing over his drum which he played in the Ilford National School Fife and Drum band. He had been in the band

In 1867 the Headteacher of the Ilford National School in Essex was called Mr Tuck. The school had a fife and drum band and every year the band led the whole school in a procession to a meadow on the site of what is now Ilford Town Hall where they would have their annual picnic.

After reading this they decided to imagine what would happen if a rebellious boy from those days met up with an unhappy girl from their own time.

for three years and was the best drummer there. Unfortunately he didn't get on with Mr Tuck, the teacher.

Every year the Ilford National Fife and Drum band had a procession through Ilford which ended with a picnic on the meadow. Ernie had always been in the procession since he had broken into the band. It was the event of the year.

Mr Tuck didn't get on with Ernie at all. He wanted him out but was unable to work out how.

On the Friday before the procession the band had a final rehearsal. Ernie was there. He was going to bang his drums loud, not for him, but because he wanted everyone to sit up and take notice.

Bang! Bang! Thump! went Ernie's drum as the fifes' noise droned away. The only thing that Mr Tuck could hear was Ernie thumping away. He stopped the band (without Ernie hearing) and went up to him. Ernie didn't know it until Mr Tuck's baton was stuck in his back.

'Ow!' he yelled, before listening to the silence.

'Did you make that noise deliberately, Toffet?'

'N n n no s s sir. I just want the b b b ... '

'Glory, Toffet, glory. You want everyone to see you, don't you?'

'N n no s s s sir.'

'Don't lie TO ME TOFFET!' exploded Tuck. 'You want to be the star. Well that's your lot, Toffet. You're out!'

'You're having me on ... '

'OUT!'

As Ernie left the room he yelled, 'I'll pay you out, Tuck! You've not seen the last of Ernie Toffet!'

For the remainder of the day Ernie plotted and schemed, plotted and schemed, and, in the end, came up with his masterplan. Then he went and saw his friend, Bert, who wasn't too well.

'How are you?' Ernie asked him.

'I'm okay. I'll be up and about tomorrow and I can see you in the band on Sunday.' He was surprised when Ernie's face dropped.

'What's up Ern?' he asked.

'Tuck's chucked me out.'

'What?'

'I told you he hated me. He's done it on purpose. He hates my guts, you should know that.'

'Yeah, but you're the best.'

'Okay, I'm good, but he can still get someone. I'm going to go and sabotage it.'

'Sabotage it? How?'

'I'm going to put jam in the fifes and cut the drum skins open. As they bang they'll go right through!'

'I wouldn't do it if I were you. Too risky.'

'Well, tough. I'm going tonight. You can't stop me, Bert.'

Ernie set off just before midnight. He arrived at Mr Tuck's house to discover something strange. It was like a carriage, but a lot smaller.

'Tuck the mad inventor,' thought Ernie. 'Now how do I get in?'

It didn't take him long to see a slightly open window on the second floor. Near to it was a pipe which went up the wall. Ernie saw this and started climbing up it.

Soon enough Ernie was up the top of the pipe. He leaned over to get to the window. He opened it up. To his surprise a bed was made up. 'Must be a spare,' he thought. He started for the door when he heard a noise from the bed. He looked towards the bed and saw a girl's face appear.

'Who are you?' she asked.

'Ernie, Ernie Toffet. What's your name, little girl?' he replied, although he had no right to use the word 'little' as she was probably taller than him.

'Anita.'

'Anita Tuck, not really a great name,' he thought out loud.

'Anita Tuck' where do you get that name?'

'Well this is Mr Tuck's house, isn't it?'

But before Anita had a chance to reply the door opened. She screamed and hid under the covers. Ernie looked around, startled.

'What are you doing, Ern?' said a voice that belonged to Bert.

'Bert! How on earth did you get here?'

'The back door was open. Now come on and get out of here or Tuck will find us.'

'But the girl … '

'What girl?'

'That girl.' Ernie pointed in her direction. However, there was no girl at the end of his finger. Instead the drum which Ernie played was there.

'Let's get going. Tuck'll find us in a minute.'

Together Ernie and Bert shinned down the pipe and walked off into the night.

*

Anita sat there, not concentrating on what Ms Godfrey was saying. She kept recalling what had happened the previous night. She was confused at what she saw. Who was he? Why was he opening the window? She needed to know the answers.

'Anita, you're not paying any attention,' said Ms Godfrey.

'Uh, oh yeah, sorry. I was … em, … thinking of something else.'

Ms Godfrey put down her chalk and walked over to Anita.

'Anita, is anything wrong? You haven't been acting yourself lately.'

'No, nothing's wrong,' Anita answered.

'Are you sure?'

Anita was getting more confused. She had to tell someone, she had to let it out.

'Anita?'

'Uh, em, yesterday, yesterday night, I was woken by a noise and I saw this ghost climbing through the window.'

'A ghost? Are you sure?'

'Positive.'

'Anita, you know that ghosts don't really exist. They're just fairy tales. You probably were just dreaming.'

'I wasn't! I know I wasn't. It really did happen.'

'Okay, calm down.'

No one said anything for a while.

'Anita, I want you to take the morning off. Go upstairs to your bedroom and have a good think over this carefully. Then when you're ready to talk again you can come and see me. All right?'

'Yeah, okay,' Anita said. Anita gathered her books and walked out. Ms Godfrey stood there with a worried expression on her face.

Anita went up to her bedroom. She flung her books on the desk and flopped onto the bed. She stared at the ceiling. 'Why doesn't anyone believe me?' she thought. 'I know it's true.'

She closed her eyes, her thoughts trailing off. Before she knew it she was fast asleep. Downstairs, Ms Godfrey was making a telephone call.

'Yes doctor … she's acting very strangely. She said she'd seen a ghost. I'm sure she's feeling ill. You must come and take a look. Yes, yes I understand. Of course. Half an hour's time. Right. Well, thank you doctor.'

'Anita, wake up. There's someone here to see you,' said Ms Godfrey.

Anita half opened her eyes.

'Mum?' she said wearily.

'No, no, it's not your mother, dear. It's a doctor, Dr. Richards.'

'Doctor?'

'Yes, a doctor. Now sit up.'

Ms Godfrey bent over Anita and made her sit up. Anita looked at the doctor.

'I don't need a doctor. There's nothing wrong with me. I'm not ill.'

'Um Ms Godfrey, would you mind waiting outside?' said the doctor.

'Yes of course.'

Ms Godfrey walked over to the door, gave a quick nod to the doctor and left.

The doctor took out a thermometer. 'Open up,' he said.

Anita opened her mouth and the doctor popped in the thermometer. After a couple of minutes the doctor took out the thermometer. He had a look at her temperature.

'Your temperature is normal.'

'My temperature is normal because there's nothing wrong with me.'

'You do look a little pale though.'

'Me, pale? I'm not. I'm perfectly all right,' cried Anita.

Dr. Richards put down his bag and looked at Anita.

'Anita, your tutor, Ms Godfrey, has been telling me that em ... you've been seeing a ghost.'

'She's told you I saw a ghost! I trusted her as well.' Anita threw off her duvet and ran towards the door. She turned round to the doctor. She was furious. 'I'M NOT ILL!' she shouted.

Anita opened the door. In front of her Ms Godfrey was standing there with a shocked face.

'How dare you talk to the doctor like that. Go and apologise at once.'

'Why should I? You should apologise to me for telling the doctor in the first place.'

By this time the doctor had packed his things and was standing by Anita. 'Anita, calm down. I just wanted to give you a check-up,' he said, sympathetically. 'Ms Godfrey was only doing what she thought was the best.'

Anita couldn't take any more. She just ran into her bedroom and slammed the door. She heard a few whispers, then silence. Anita was now more determined to meet the ghost. She decided to wait up for the ghost.

Hours went by and Anita refused to eat anything and was feeling tired. She occupied herself by reading a book. Anita could see it was getting dark. She began to doze off. All of a sudden Anita heard the window creak. Anita was scared. She looked towards the window. She saw someone climbing through it.

'Who's there?' she whispered.

'Ernie, Ernie Toffet,' he said, staring at Anita. 'Who are you? What are you doing here?'

'I'm Anita ... '

'Anita, what was that noise? Are you all right?' It was Ms Godfrey and her footsteps were getting closer and closer.

'Oh no, it's Ms Godfrey,' said Anita. Just at that moment the door was flung open.

'Anita, what was that noise? What's happening?'

Anita didn't know what to say. 'I saw him ... Ernie.'

'Ernie? Who's Ernie?'

Anita pointed towards the window. 'There. Look,' she said.

'There's nothing there,' Ms Godfrey said, her beady eyes searching the room. 'You've been dreaming again.'

Anita looked towards the window. Ms Godfrey was right. No one was there. 'But I saw him. He was right there!'

'Well he's not there now,' said Ms Godfrey. She went over to the bed and put her hand across Anita's forehead. 'I knew it. Your forehead is very hot. I just knew you were ill.' Ms Godfrey tucked Anita in. 'I'll be back in a minute. I'm going to get you some medicine.' Ms Godfrey left.

'Where's Ernie?' she said to herself. 'Why do you keep disappearing?' Anita took a final look at the window. She got out of bed and walked to the window. She was puzzled, very puzzled. What did he want? Where was he?

1 What does the story tell you about Ernie and about Anita? Do you think Mr Tuck is right when he says that all Ernie is interested in is glory? How do you think Anita feels about her tutor?

2 So far in this story Ernie has found his way into Anita's time. What do you think would happen if Anita found her way back into Ernie's time? Do you think she would help Ernie? If so, how?

Writing Your Own Time-slip Story

1 In groups of two or three write your own time-slip story, using either Tom or Ernie as one of your characters from the past.

Starting Writing

Choose a character from the present day to meet either Tom or Ernie. S/He could be a real person or somebody you have made up, but not yourself.

Decide where the meeting is going to take place and how you are going to lead up to the moment of time-slip.

Decide how the characters will react to each other and how they will affect each other's lives.

Decide which part of the story each group member is going to write

Composing

Do a first draft of your part of the story.

Revising

Read it to the others. Together, make sure that the different parts of the story fit. Look particularly at the way the characters speak and behave to each other.

Proof-reading

Check your spelling and punctuation. Use a dictionary.

Make a final draft and type or wordprocess it.

Publishing

Each read part of it to the whole class.

You might like to make a class display of your story.

Reflection

In this Unit you have been practising how to:

- *write a book review for a newspaper*
- *plan and write a holiday brochure*
- *take part in a role play*
- *use language to convey ideas*
- *read and understand an extract from a novel*
- *write a story with a given character and period*
- *write a story with a clear structure*

Talk to your friends and your teacher about the things you have been doing in this Unit. Decide how much you have understood and how much progress you have made. Filling in Unit 6 of the Record Sheet on page 84 will also help you think about what you have done in this Unit and the knowledge you are gaining in your English lessons.

Important: Your teacher will give you photocopied versions of these two pages so that you do not need to write in this book.

First of all, with a friend, talk about and decide what the short statements mean. Discuss what you have been practising in English and how much you have understood of what you have done.

Next to each statement there are three targets to aim for. This is what they mean:

I understand this and have practised it.

I have done this with help.

I feel able to do this again.

If you are not sure what a statement means or whether you can do what it says, discuss it with your teacher.

Put a tick under the target that you think best describes what you can do. If you are in doubt, please ask for help.

Name of Student

I can

Unit 4
ask and answer questions about poems

take part in a group presentation

express my personal views about poems

read poems aloud

say which poems I prefer and why

work out the meaning of a poem

find and choose poems from a library

read a range of poetry

revise and draft poems

write different kinds of poems

assemble ideas on a wordprocessor

use words in a deliberate order in a poem

Unit 5
take part in a role play

use language to convey ideas

read and understand an extract from a novel

write a story, with a given character and period

write a story with a clear structure

Unit 6
respond positively to other people's ideas

show I can understand the meaning of letters and newspaper articles

select reference materials for a newspaper article

express my own views on what I have read

show how a writer's choice of words affects the message

write a letter to a newspaper

write a newspaper article

write a book review for a newspaper

plan and write a holiday brochure

			Other comments

Thinking Back

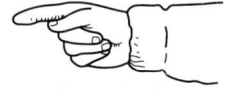

◆ Which is the best piece of work that you have done so far? Why do you think it was particularly successful?

◆ Which of the work in the last three Units did you enjoy most?

◆ What have you learned about language that you did not know before?

◆ Was there anything you did not understand and would like more help with?

Thinking Forward

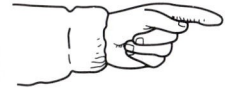

◆ Where do you think you need to improve most? What can you do to help you do so?

◆ What kind of activities can you suggest to your teacher that you could do as extra work?

This Unit gives you the opportunity to

- find out how drama began
- play different roles
- read and produce a radio play
- write and 'broadcast' a radio play
- use a tape-recorder

Operation Airwaves is an opportunity for you to explore what it would be like to work in a radio station. Before you do so there is a cartoon history of drama for you to study which will help you to understand how plays have developed over many years.

..To be or not to be...

Perhaps the most famous writer of all times – William Shakespeare

In Europe street plays of all kinds were popular

People have always acted

The Romans added a stage

The Greeks staged plays as part of festivals and games

Before the invention of television people went to popular plays in the theatre

"A flower girl would never have married him!"

At the start of this century plays were full of new ideas

TO BE OR NOT TO BE...

The BBC was formed in 1927 and soon after radio plays began to be written

The invention of television has taken drama into new areas again

Producing a Radio Play

Imagine that you are a team of people working in the Drama Department of a national radio station. Your team has been sent *The Midas Factor*, a script which has been selected by the Youth Drama Unit to be broadcast.

1 Get into groups of seven or eight. Your job is to produce this play.

09.00 It is nine o'clock in the morning. The production team are meeting to cast, rehearse and then broadcast *The Midas Factor*.

Decide on your jobs. Six of you are going to be actors. One of you will be the producer, one the technician (the person who does the sound effects.) You may need to do more than one job if there are only seven in your group.

09.10 You are now going to have your first read-through of the script. The producer will decide who reads which part. (This may well be changed later on.) S/he also makes notes on things that will need to be raised at the script conference after the reading. These might include the way actors should say lines, possible ideas for making sound effects, etc. The technician should read out the sound cues which are in capital letters in brackets.

The Midas Factor

Characters

Jessica – a young woman

Reg – the factory caretaker, an old man

Jo

Alan

Mark } workers in the factory

Norah

(INTERIOR. SOUND OF MACHINERY. FOOTSTEPS GETTING LOUDER, THEN STOPPING.)

REG: Just a minute.

(SOUND OF HEAVY DOOR OPENING AND SHUTTING. SOUND OF MACHINERY STOPS. ACOUSTIC INDICATES SMALL ROOM.)

REG: Okay Jessica you can take the blindfold off now.

JESSICA: Where am I?

REG: In a store room.

JESSICA: But I've never been in here before.

REG: It isn't often used

JESSICA: What is all this about? Why did I have to wear a blindfold?

REG: Jessica I want you to meet some friends of mine.

JESSICA: But I know everyone here ...

REG: Are you sure?

JESSICA: Of course I'm sure? It's the other people from the factory. Here's Alan ...

ALAN: The great Alonzo, if you don't mind.

(SOUND OF THREE PEOPLE CLAPPING)

JESSICA: I beg your pardon.

ALAN: Conjuror, magician and all-round entertainer.

JO: Take no notice of him. All he ever did was perform at children's parties. Now I was a real actor.

JESSICA: You, Jo?

JO: Josephine Labouche, at your service.

(SOUND OF WOLF-WHISTLING AND CHEERING)

JESSICA: Labouche?

NORAH: That was her stage name. Her real name is Josie Brown.

JO: An actress has a right to choose a name that suits her.

NORAH: Listen to her, giving herself airs.

JO: We all give ourselves airs. That's what it's about.

JESSICA: And were you an actress, too, Norah?

ALAN: She was not.

NORAH: I was a puppeteer.

ALAN: A string-puller.

NORAH: Better than pulling rabbits out of hats.

MARK: Whereas I have trod the boards in every theatre, in every town in England.

NORAH: Listen to Mark.

MARK: 'To be, or not to be, that is the question.' Shakespeare, my dear.

NORAH: He's never even read a play by Shakespeare.

MARK: I most certainly have.

JO: I was Lady Macbeth.

JESSICA: Who's she?

JO: Oh, you poor girl. Such ignorance.

(THEY BEGIN TALKING AT THE SAME TIME, INTERRUPTING EACH OTHER)

NORAH: You should have seen my Punch and Judy.

JESSICA: Your what?

MARK: 'Friends, Romans and countrymen, lend me your ears.'

ALAN: Pick a card, any card, I don't care. Don't let me see it.

JESSICA: Wait! Please! One at a time.

REG: Stop! The poor girl can't think straight. I must apologise for my companions, Jessica. You see, they haven't met someone like you for a very long time.

JESSICA: But what do you mean? There's nothing special about me.

NORAH: Oh yes there is.

JESSICA: What?

JO: Can't you guess?

JESSICA: No.

ALAN: What every entertainer needs.

MARK: Quite simply ...

JO: In a word ...

REG: An audience.

JESSICA: An audience. What's that?

REG: Oh dear. I suppose we'd better start at the beginning.

JESSICA: Please do.

REG: Why don't you all sit down.

(SOUND OF CHAIRS SCRAPING ON THE FLOOR.)

REG: You see only about thirty years ago, before you were born of course, this place wasn't a factory at all.

JESSICA: Then what was it?

NORAH: It was a theatre!

JESSICA: What's that?

JO: A place where people came to be entertained.

JESSICA: But that's against the law.

MARK: It is now.

ALAN: It wasn't always.

REG: Before the food crisis.

NORAH: Before the fuel riots.

JO: Before the emergency government.

JESSICA: Before everyone had to work so hard?

REG: That's right.

JO: That was when life was glorious.

JESSICA: But people then were terribly lazy.

ALAN: That's what they told you at school.

JESSICA: They only worked about eight hours a day.

MARK: Isn't that enough?

JESSICA: But the country didn't earn enough money.

NORAH: So we're told.

JESSICA: We have to make enough money to meet everybody's needs. That's why we must always work harder.

REG: Is that why we all have to work fifteen hours a day, Jessica? To meet our needs?

NORAH: Or is it to satisfy our rulers' greed?

JESSICA: You mustn't say that. Our ruler thinks of nothing else but making the people happy.

REG: Our ruler thinks of nothing else but money!

JESSICA: (*Shocked*) How can you say that!

REG: Very easily. You see I can remember what it used to be like.

JO: The good old days!

(SOUND OF CIRCUS MUSIC.)

ALAN: (*Shouting*) We were all entertainers then.

MARK: (*Shouting*) Entertainers and artistes.

JO: (*Shouting*) Actors and actresses.

(MUSIC FADES.)

REG: (*Sadly*) Yes, the good old days!

JESSICA: What did you do Reg?

NORAH: He gave orders all day long.

REG: I was the director. The hardest job of all.

JO: I don't think!

JESSICA: And what about ... ? What did you call it? My job?

MARK: The audience.

JESSICA: What did the audience do?

(SOUND OF AUDIENCE IN LARGE HALL, TALKING, COUGHING, BLOWING NOSES, RUSTLING SWEET PAPERS)

NORAH: You sat and watched.

JESSICA: Is that all?

ALAN: There's more to it than that.

JESSICA: Such as?

ALAN: Well, the audience had to think. They had to use their minds.

(SOUND OF AUDIENCE CLAPPING)

JO: Not when *you* were performing.

(SOUND OF AUDIENCE BOOING AND JEERING)

JESSICA: But didn't the audience actually do anything else apart from just sit there?

MARK: Well at the end you clapped.

JESSICA: Clapped?

MARK: You sort of hit your hands together, like this.

(SOUND OF ONE PERSON CLAPPING)

REG: Quietly! Someone might hear you.

JESSICA: But what would I do that for?

MARK: To show you liked the play of course.

JESSICA: What's a play?

MARK: Oh this is hopeless!

JO: It's like talking to the wall.

JESSICA: I'm sorry, I do want to know. It's just ... all these new words. I don't know what they mean.

MARK: A play is when you pretend to be someone else.

JESSICA: Pretend to be someone else. But what's the point of that?

REG: Well, let's show her, shall we?

JO: What, now?

REG: Why not?

MARK: Suppose someone comes.

REG: We can go back to working the machines.

ALAN: It's very risky.

JESSICA: Oh yes, please. I'd love to see a ... what did you call it?

REG: A play.

JESSICA: Yes.

REG: All right then. We'll do it. But first we need a story.

JESSICA: A story. I don't ...

REG: Yes, we know. You don't know what that is either. Don't worry. You'll find out. Let's show her what happens when you get too fond of money.

JESSICA: I hope it won't say anything bad about our ruler.

REG: Of course not. This is a play about someone else altogether, about a King who lived long long ago. He was called King Midas. Okay everyone, let's show Jessica what else we can do apart from pushing buttons and pulling levers.

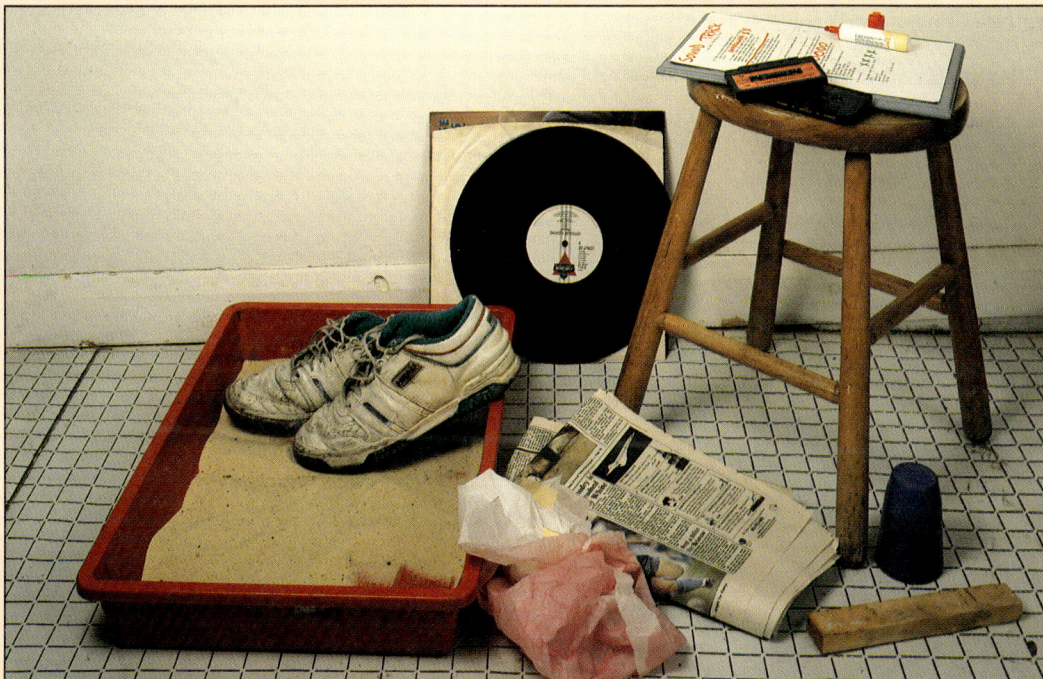

9.25 The production team now meets together to discuss the play. Everybody contributes his or her opinion about how it sounded.

9.35 Final casting takes place. This involves a team discussion with the producer having the final say.

9.45 The group now divides up into two groups.

The actors go off to the rehearsal area to read through the play as a group and then practise it individually.

The producer and technician work together in the studio area. They go through the script deciding how they will do the sound effects. They adapt the writer's sound cues, making any necessary changes depending on the equipment that they have.

Some time later
When all those involved in the performance of the play are ready, the producer calls them together for a final rehearsal with sound effects.

The play is performed and the producer makes helpful comments to each of the actors. These will refer to such things as :

◆ whether every word can be heard

◆ how actors are playing their characters

◆ if sound effects are right

◆ if there are any changes or improvements that need to be made to the script. These could include extra sound effects or music.

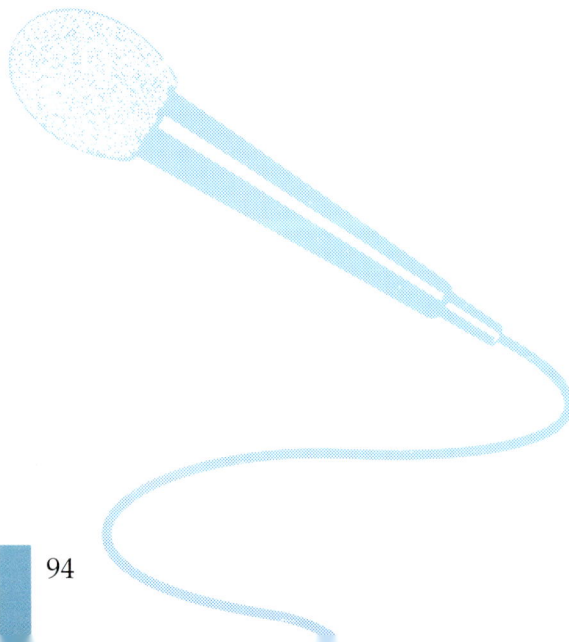

When all the necessary preparations are complete, the producer will arrange the final recording. This can be done as one whole play or as a number of 'takes' or sections. Before you make your recording, listen to a radio play and hear how they start and finish. Note especially how you find out which actors are playing the parts.

Later still
The play is 'broadcast' to other groups in the school.

In your groups decide what are the differences between performing a play for radio and reading a play aloud in class. What are the differences between 'acting' on the radio and 'acting' on the stage? Does performing a play on the radio have any advantages over performing it on stage?

The Midas Factor is so popular that your team is asked to write a sequel or follow-up to it, continuing from where Pat O'Halloran left off.

In groups, or individually if you prefer, write another episode suitable for recording and broadcasting to people of your own age.

Use the advice sheet opposite to help you.

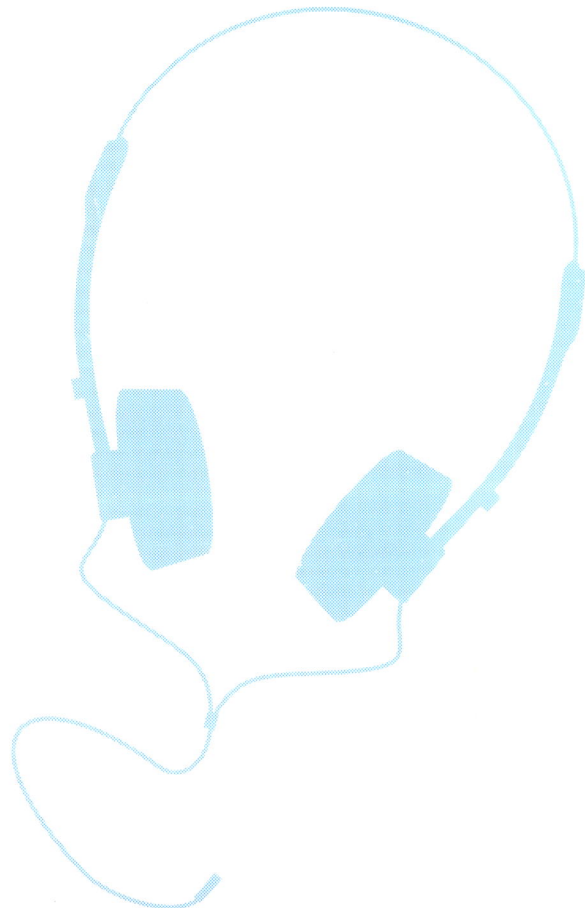

OPERATION
Airwaves

Advice for young radio writers

1. Remember that the only scenery for radio plays is the scenery you will create in the minds of your listeners. You have to describe everything you want listeners to know using words and sounds.

2. Good radio plays are difficult to write so don't worry if your first attempt needs redrafting!

3. There are no scenes in a radio play.

4. Describe your sound effects clearly. Try not to use too many sounds or your listeners may become confused. Set them out in capital letters in brackets.

5. Take care to refer to your characters by name often as your audience cannot see them!

6. Set out your script as in the specimen script (**The Midas Factor**) which is attached to this advice sheet. Some writers find it helpful to number each speech on each page to help the producer and actors when rehearsing.

Reflection

In this Unit you have been practising how to

- *plan and take part in a presentation (a radio play)*
- *contribute to a discussion about a play*
- *read a part in a play*
- *write a radio play*
- *set out a radio play correctly*

Talk to your friends and your teacher about the things you have been doing in this Unit. Decide how much you have understood and how much progress you have made. Filling in Unit 7 of the Record Sheet on page 118 will also help you think about what you have done in this Unit and the knowledge you are gaining in your English lessons.

Unit 8 Operation Airwaves 2

This Unit gives you the opportunity to

● *present your ideas and opinions*
● *recognise the difference between fact and opinion*
● *present information in a lively way*
● *play a role*
● *plan and take part in a presentation*
● *research information*

The people who think up radio programmes are always on the lookout for new ideas. They are particularly interested in attracting young listeners.

Listening Habits

In small groups, use this questionnaire, which also appears as a repromaster in the *Teacher's Resource Book*, to find out the listening habits of your class.

Radio Questionnaire

1 How often do you listen to the radio?

never ☐   sometimes ☐   every day ☐

2 Which radio station do you listen to?

Radio 1 ☐   Radio 2 ☐   Radio 3 ☐   Radio 4 ☐   Radio 5 ☐

Local radio *e.g. Capital* ....(please write name)

Others ....

3 What kind of programmes do you listen to?

news ☐   'children's' ☐   pop music ☐

other music ☐   features ☐

Others ....

4 If a new radio station was being set up especially for young people, what subjects do you think it should produce programmes about? (i.e. what do you feel strongly about and want to hear on the radio?)

5 Have you any complaints to make about radio programmes for young people?

Interview with Mary Kalemkerian, Radio Producer

1 Study this interview with Mary Kalemkerian, a producer of young people's programmes for BBC Radio.

How long have you been working in Children's Radio?

Twelve years. I started in Radio Scotland on the first children's programme they had had since the old days of *Listen With Mother* in the nineteen-fifties.

What is your job now?

I'm Chief Producer of Children's Magazines for Radio Five.

When they hear the word 'magazines' most people think of things you buy in a newsagent's shop. What do you mean by it?

I mean magazine programmes, programmes that are full of short items, music and features, joined seamlessly together with music, usually with a serial which is normally someone reading a story.

Could you just explain that word 'features'?

A feature is a piece of radio wrapped around a topic.

What do you think of what's on offer for young people now on the radio?

I think it's terrible. Apart from Radio One, which a lot of young people listen to, there is very little for them. We're hoping to change that. We're bringing out a magazine show that is one and a half hours long every day of the holidays.

Do you think some age groups are served better than others?

It's best to try to avoid thinking too much in age groups. Just do what you think is interesting.

But there are differences between children's programmes and adults' programmes, aren't there?

Oh yes. The items tend to be shorter in children's programmes. They tend to have a shorter attention span. You've got to get their interest straight away.

Can we talk about what's involved in making a magazine programme? For example, how many people are there in your team?

At the moment there's the Chief Producer – that's me, three producers, two researchers, one reporter, a production assistant, one programme manager and a presenter. And we usually get someone in to read the story.

What do they all do? For example, where do the ideas for the programme come from?

Generally from the producers. Sometimes the researchers come up with ideas as well.

So the producer has an idea, how does it get turned into a feature?

Well, the producer will ask the researcher to find out background information, come up with musical ideas, that sort of thing. For example, if we were doing a feature on birthdays, the researcher would be checking out what famous people had their birthdays on this day.

What else might the researcher do?

Making up quizzes and competitions, looking all the time for what is happening. They'll be reading teenage magazines, books, looking at television.

What about the reporter?

She or he will be doing interviews, news reports, going to places where something has happened. Sometimes the researchers might do that as well if there's a lot of reporting that needs to be done.

And the production assistant?

She or he will be coping with all the paperwork. There's an enormous amount of it. Every bit of music, for example, has to be listed and timed so that everybody in the team knows exactly what is going to be in the programme. The production assistant will be dealing a lot with studio time, working with a stop-watch, typing up scripts, dealing with letters.

And what about the programme manager?

That's a new job. He or she will be overseeing all the technical matters. The production manager will usually have a technical training.

That's not the same as your job then?

No. I deal with editorial matters.

Can you explain that?

Well, I'm working with the producers on the content of the programme, developing ideas, making sure that everything is current, up-to-date. For example, if you're dealing with the music business it changes all the time; you can't afford to be talking about something that was big news last month.

2 Do you think Mary Kalemkerian understands young people?

What does she think makes a good radio programme? Make a list of the things she says. Put them into your own order of importance.

Does she answer any of the complaints that you made when you answered the questionnaire?

you have any advice for children ing to make their own magazine gramme?

ep the items short. Get a good variety stuff. Think of good ways of linking it. major serial is quite nice. Have plenty of nour. Get an interesting guest, neone who's got something to say. A star has not always got the most eresting things to say. There may be neone in your local area that's a real aracter. Start off with your own area, re may be someone in your own ool or club. Use music imaginatively, ak pieces up with little bits of music. t a variety of interesting voices, young ces, older voices, different accents. Try give your listener a bit of surprise now then. Use sound effects. If you've got kid telling a story get another kid to ke up some sound effects to go with Get the best kid presenting. I don't an the cleverest.

hat does make a good presenter en?

ll, you have to let your personality ne over. You've got to sound natural en though you're not being natural. u have to imagine you're talking to person not to a huge audience, agine you're talking to a friend, ture that person.

there anything a presenter should oid?

ll, I listen to some of the local tions and I often think the presenters

sound a bit manic.

What do you mean by manic?

They seem to be shouting a lot.

Anything else?

Well obviously you've got to avoid talking down to people, especially children. I think they sometimes do that on Radio One. I was listening to a presenter the other day and he sounded as if he was trying to pretend he was about ten. I don't think that's a good idea. You have to sound confident and natural.

What do you think the future of radio is going to be like? Do you feel that it is in competition with television?

Very good. We have had to learn from TV. We have to be as immediate as they are on TV and I think we can do that. I think that radio can be more accessible. We can put people on the air much more easily. It's not such a complicated process. You can listen to radio while you're walking around or driving around. You can carry it with you. I also think that people tend to feel that the radio presenter is talking directly to them. You don't feel that so much with TV. You don't feel that the presenter is having a conversation with you.

3 Here are some topics suggested by people of your own age that could be used to make better radio programmes.

Animal Rights, Quizzes, Young People Singing, Soap-Opera, Under-Age Smoking, Help With Homework, News, Jokes, Interviews With Famous People, Match Commentaries, Phone-Ins,

Problems With Friends And Parents, Drama Acted By Young People, The Environment.

Which of these do you agree with? Do they make you think of any others?

In a survey carried out for this book the most popular topic was Animal Rights.

Imagine that you are a team of people making a Magazine Programme for a radio station of your choice. Your team has been told to produce a lively new show to go out to young people on Saturday mornings. Audience research has come up with this list of ingredients for the first programme.

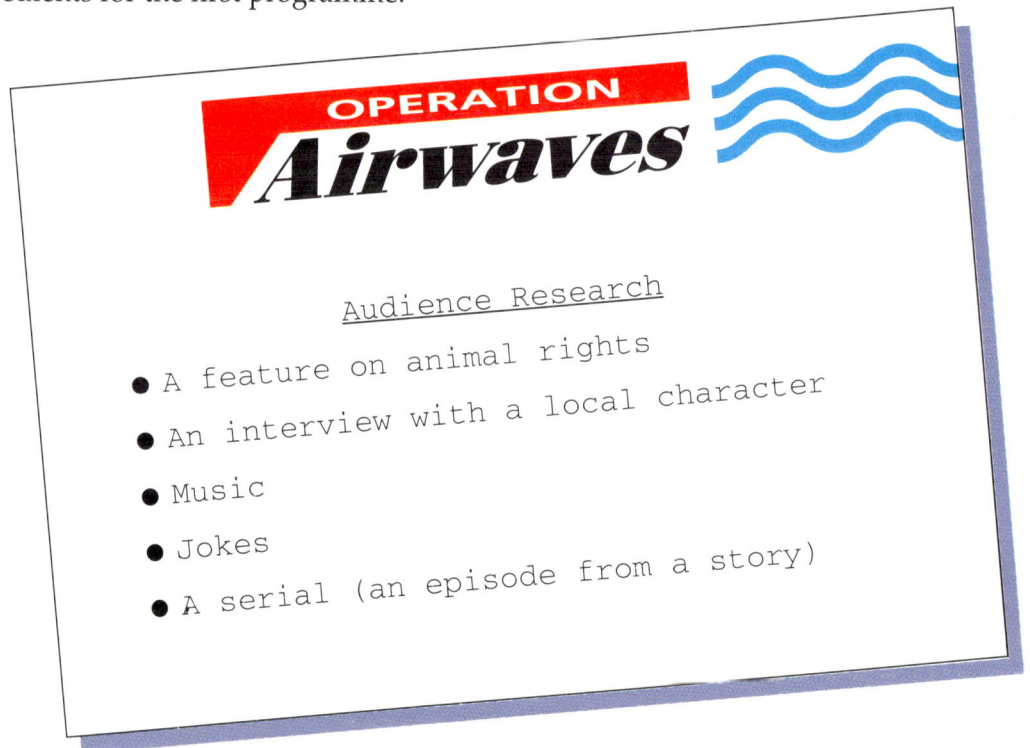

OPERATION Airwaves

Audience Research

- A feature on animal rights
- An interview with a local character
- Music
- Jokes
- A serial (an episode from a story)

1 Get into small groups. Your job is to research, rehearse and broadcast a twenty minute magazine programme for young people. You will need to go through the following stages.

- ◆ Sharing ideas.
- ◆ Researching material.
- ◆ Putting your ideas into practice.
- ◆ Rehearsing and timing.
- ◆ Going on air.

09.00 It is nine o'clock in the morning and you are meeting to plan the programme. Think of a good snappy title for it. A certain amount of material has already been provided by the station's research library. Read what they have come up with. Some of it is fact, it is definitely true; some of it is opinion, what people think about a topic. Your feature will need to contain both of these kinds of information but it should make clear which is which.

Animals ... are there merely as a means to an end. That end is man
Immanuel Kant.

A hundred times as many animals are killed to eat as are used in experiments.
Research Scientist.

Beauty and the beast

In many countries, companies are compelled by law to test all new chemical products on animals. Lipsticks, toothpastes, shampoos and weedkillers undergo extensive testing to assess their potential side-effects on humans. Some of these tests have been criticised by scientists, either for being unreliable when their results are applied to humans, or because they use unnecessarily large numbers of animals. The LD50 test is especially criticised for these reasons. LD stands for lethal dose and in the experiment a chemical is injected in increasing amounts until 50 per cent of the animals die.

Increasingly, consumers are choosing products which have not been tested on animals. This has led some manufacturers to investigate alternative testing techniques. However, the use of animals for testing cosmetics and other non-medical products accounts for only a small proportion of animal experiments.

The Draize test, in which the chemical is dropped into the eye of a rabbit, is routinely used to test shampoos. Scientists are trying to find alternative testing methods, for example the use of cell cultures (cells from animals kept outside the body), and the use of computer models. But so far, the Draize test has not been successfully replaced.

Testing on animals
The diagram shows the percentage of different types of research which use animals. The majority of experiments are in the fields of medical and veterinary research and have led to improvements in the quality of life for *both* people and animals. Only a small proportion of animal experiments involve the testing of cosmetics. However, many people argue that there are plenty of cosmetics and shampoos on the market and that the testing of new products involves unnecessary suffering.

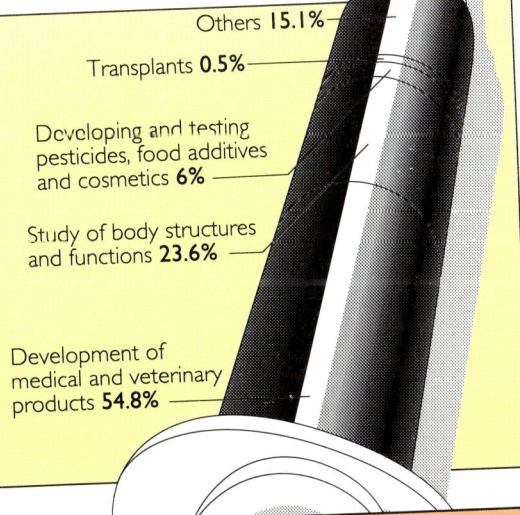

Others **15.1%**

Transplants **0.5%**

Developing and testing pesticides, food additives and cosmetics **6%**

Study of body structures and functions **23.6%**

Development of medical and veterinary products **54.8%**

Animal testing is the only known way to make sure products are safe.
Research Chemist.

Blood sports

Blood sports have always been popular and in some countries they are an important part of the people's tradition and culture. Falconry and deer hunting go back thousands of years while fox hunting and hare coursing began much more recently. Shooting as a sport is widely practised throughout Europe and North America – thousands of pigeons, pheasants and ducks are shot each year.

Animal welfare groups argue that blood sports should be banned. They also say that hunting with hounds is worse than shooting because of the distress caused by the chase. The hunters, however, claim their sport is justified as the culling, reducing the numbers, of species such as deer and foxes is necessary; people have removed the animals' natural predators and provided them with extra food through farming. They also point out that large areas of land have been preserved for wildlife because of hunting.

In Europe and North America there has recently been an upsurge in illegal dog-fighting and badger-baiting and raccoon-baiting. Bull terriers are placed in rings with either another dog, or a badger, to fight to death while spectators bet heavily on the winner. Sports like cock-fighting which involve pitting one animal against another are also banned in much of the West – but they are still very popular in the Far East.

Every year thousands of bulls and hundreds of horses are killed or maimed in Spanish bullrings and in the arenas of France, Portugal, Mexico and South America. In Spain alone bullfighting is estimated to be a $100 million industry and has great cultural importance. But does this justify the continued and persistent infliction of pain on the animal for the pleasure of the spectators?

"How smart does a chimpanzee have to be before killing him constitutes murder?"
Dr. Carl Sagan

"Farm animals today are better looked after than they ever were"
National Union of Farmers

Children often tease their pets and, without realising, cause them suffering. Pets also suffer deliberate ill-treatment. Thousands of puppies and kittens are abandoned each year. In Britain 137,632 unwanted pets were destroyed in 1985 and the situation in the USA is believed to be worse. It has been estimated that one-third of the American dog population ends up in animal shelters.

"The battery hen is the most miserable creature in the feathered world."
Lord Houghton.

103

"Elephants standing on their front legs is unnatural and proven cruelty."
Veterinary Surgeon.

THE RESPONSIBLE WAY FORWARD IN BODYCARE

The macaque monkey

Several species of macaque are used in research. In some establishments they are bred in large outdoor cages, but many thousands are still imported from the Philippines and other parts of Asia each year. In the laboratory they are housed in metal cages either singly or in groups. Macaque monkeys have been used in the development of new drugs for treating epilepsy. Other experiments on the workings of the brain using these animals have been criticised.

The armadillo

After humans, this is the next largest mammal to contract leprosy. For this reason it is now used to produce a vaccine against the disease which infects 15 million people worldwide.

As many as 750 doses can be produced from the organs of one animal and armadillos are now being specially bred for this purpose.

The chimpanzee

There are 1,200 chimpanzees currently held in research establishments throughout the world. Despite being an endangered species, chimps are usually caught in the wild because they are difficult to breed in captivity. The arrival of the disease AIDS could lead to an increase in their use as it affects them in a very similar way to humans. A European pharmaceuticals company was recently found to be keeping chimps in cages too small for them to stand upright, causing unnecessary stress.

THE RESPONSIBLE WAY FORWARD IN BODYCARE

Our industry is committed to the ultimate elimination of animal testing and shares public concern about the use of animals in the safety assessment of cosmetic and toiletry products.

We are also committed to the highest possible standards of consumer and employee safety and have an excellent record in this area.

The majority of our products are made from ingredients which have a known safety record. Neither the ingredients nor the products require animal testing.

The need for animal testing arises primarily with the introduction of new ingredients. Only when all available and validated non-animal alternatives have been used and some human safety concern remains is animal testing considered. The benefits from new ingredients include:

- Human health, for example anti-plaque/tartar agents, UV filters;
- Human safety, for example preservative systems;
- Environmental improvement such as biodegradability.

Such benefits must be weighed against the consumer's wish to have products which do not use animals in their safety testing.

THE 3 R's POLICY

REDUCE – REFINE – REPLACE

The industry believes the responsible way forward is to provide products which meet the newly emerging consumer safety and environmental demands but to do so in the context of the "3 R's" policy.

TO REDUCE

the need for animal testing to an absolute minimum. Major contributions have been made in this area in the last few years and more progress is anticipated.

TO REFINE

the tests to make them more acceptable, both by refinement of methods and reduction in the number of animals involved per test.

TO REPLACE

the tests using live animals by alternative methods thus eliminating all animal testing. This can be done through better management of information and the development of alternative testing.

To focus efforts on the search for alternatives the CTPA is working closely with FRAME (Fund for the Replacement of Animals in Medical Experiments). The CTPA and its members are committed to making significant and further progress towards this goal.

Some companies have a policy whereby they will not use any new ingredient which has involved animal testing. As European Community legislation requires animal testing in some circumstances this limits the range of products which these companies can introduce, particularly in relation to active or new ingredients.

Our products include toothpaste, deodorants, soaps, skin and hair care preparations as well as colour cosmetics and perfume. These contribute to personal hygiene and improve the general quality of well being.

The industry is dedicated to providing consumers with better, safer and more environmentally acceptable products without animal testing. The way forward is by the development, validation and regulatory acceptance of non-animal alternatives. All companies within our industry support the need for such alternative tests and the industry contributes substantial sums of money to further this objective.

Within the realistic context of the "3 R's" policy, progress is being made towards the ultimate goal of the elimination of animal testing.

"We need much tighter controls on the sort of animals that can be kept as pets."
RSPCA

"Fishing is the most cruel of all the blood-sports."
Anti-Blood-Sports Campaigner.

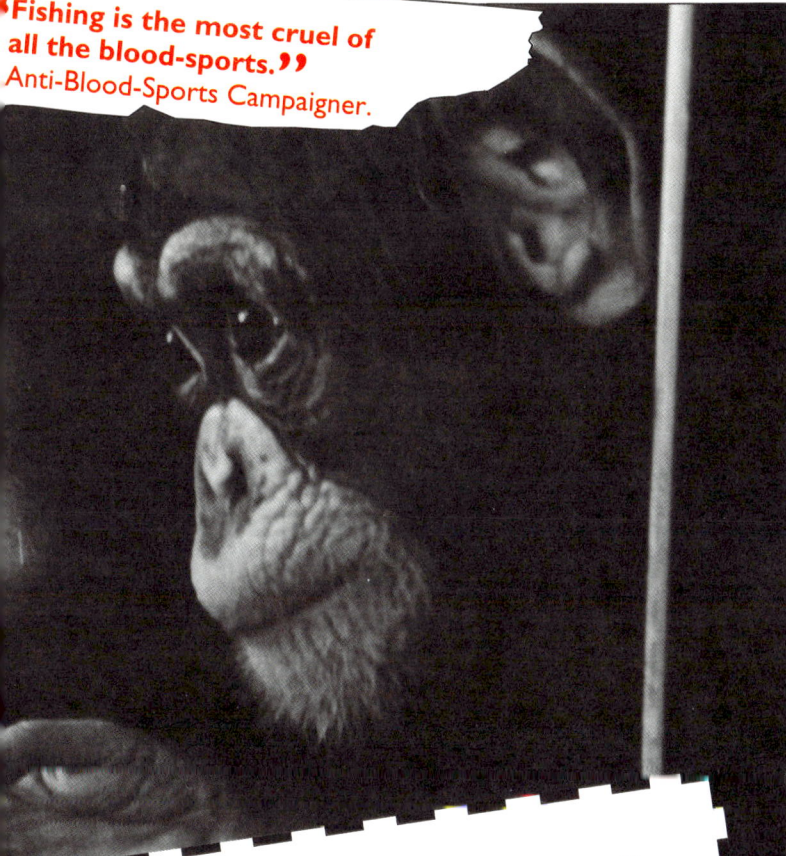

THE LAW STILL ALLOWS PEOPLE TO SQUIRT WEEDKILLER IN A BABY'S EYES, INJECT IT WITH POISON, GROW CANCERS ON ITS BACK, BURN ITS SKIN OFF, EXPOSE IT TO RADIATION AND EVENTUALLY KILL IT, IN UNRELIABLE EXPERIMENTS.

SO LONG AS IT'S ONLY AN ANIMAL.

We can prove that experiments on animals are as misleading and unproductive as they are inhuman and sickeningly cruel.
Indeed, important life saving medical advances such as blood transfusions have actually been delayed for many years by such experiments.
So write to us now for the evidence. It might make you feel sick. But it'll also make you want to help.

Name
Address

Please post to: National Anti-Vivisection Society Ltd, 51 Harley Street, London W1N 1DD.

NATIONAL ANTI-VIVISECTION SOCIETY

Working as a Team

09.15 Making decisions Your first task is to decide who will take responsibility for each part of the programme. It is important to make sure that the work is divided fairly. (You might like to look back at the interview with Mary Kalemkerian on pages 97–99 to remind yourself of what is involved. However, a team of programme-makers like yourselves, without the huge resources of the BBC, will probably find you have to help with each other's jobs!)

09.25 Your next job is to decide what is going into the programme. So far all that has been decided is that one part of the programme will be a feature on animal rights. The rest of it may have nothing to do with animals, unless you choose to make it. You will need to decide:

◆ What other material about animal rights you will use.

◆ Who you are going to interview

◆ What music to include.

◆ How you are going to include humour. (You will want to be careful about when you bring it in.)

◆ Which story you are going to make into a serial.

09.40 The research phase Go and prepare the material for the part of the programme you are working on.

OPERATION Airwaves

Running Order

Programme ....

Item Nº	Description of item	Presenter(s)	Length

Some time later

Production meeting Each member of the team describes their progress so far, presents the material they have gathered and shares any problems they have encountered. At this stage you have to decide on the running order of items in your programme.

When you have decided on the running order, you will need to time each of your items and make a note of the length. You may have to trim some items and expand others in order to fit the length of time available. Copy and use this running order sheet, which also appears as a repromaster in the *Teacher's Resource Book*, to help you.

Later still

Rehearsal Run through your programme, recording and timing it. Afterwards listen to the recording and discuss what could have been improved. You may need to rehearse your show more than once.

On air Tape-record your programme and 'broadcast' it to the rest of your class.

2 In your groups, decide what the differences are between magazine programmes and a news broadcast. For example, are there any subjects which you might find on the news but not on a magazine programme? What are the differences between the kind of interview you find in a magazine programme and the kind of interview you hear in the news?

Reflection

In this Unit you have been practising how to

- *ask and respond to questions*
- *contribute ideas to a discussion*
- *use language to convey information effectively*
- *show that you understand fact and opinion*
- *organise information into a list*
- *take part in a group presentation*

Talk to your friends and your teacher about the things you have been doing in this Unit. Decide how much you have understood and how much progress you have made. Filling in Unit 8 of the Record Sheet on page 118 will also help you think about what you have done in this Unit and the knowledge you are gaining in your English lessons.

This Unit gives you the opportunity to

● *read news stories*
● *listen to a news bulletin*
● *play different roles*
● *conduct an interview*
● *carry out some research*
● *prepare your own news bulletin*
● *use a tape-recorder*

1 In small groups look at these questions. **Brainstorm** all your thoughts and ideas about them. Brainstorming means coming up with all the ideas you can about something and making a note of them. It is important not to worry about how true they are, how well they answer a question or even whether they are sensible. What you are doing is opening up your mind.

◆ What sort of events do you hear and see reported on the radio or television news?

◆ What sort of differences are there between local and national news? Give examples to explain your views.

◆ What sort of events are not reported on

local news

national news

international news?

◆ Why do you think there are differences between local and national news?

Study these stories from newspapers. They all appeared during one month.

Girls are fuming

REBELLIOUS teenage girls are shrugging off health warnings and smoking more.

But there has been a long-term decline in the number of adults who smoke – 30 per cent were still puffing away in 1988.

There is mounting pressure to raise excise duty on tobacco to send the figure even lower.

Instant a girl struck Queen in face

THE Queen reels back, hit by a flag hurled by a protester as a celebration in New Zealand turns ugly.

A young Maori woman broke through security men to get within feet of the royal car as the Queen and Prince Philip were driven to a ceremony marking the 150th anniversary of the treaty between Britain and Maori tribes.

The Queen was visibly shocked as the woman was caught by bystanders and led away by police.

The royal car drove on to the ceremony while the Queen gathered her composure.

But hundreds of Maori protesters carrying banners marked "150 years of oppression" interrupted her speech with shouts of: "Go home, go home."

Thames on red alert

A RED alert, the most important flood warning, was in operation along the swollen Thames this week.

It means the threat of flooding to property in low-lying areas near the river.

After further rainfall, the Thames was expected to gradually rise again by the weekend.

But a National Rivers Authority area official was keen to stress that the situation was not like Gloucester, where the Severn had burst its banks.

Thames region public relations manager Jean Harper added on Wednesday: "The Thames has levelled off. It's not rising any more.

"However, because of the weather we have had last (Tuesday) you will see tain rise in the Thames, an inch or so," she added

She said that people in lying flooded areas ne river should start rem valuables upstairs.

Rainfall has a d action on the river leve Ms Harper. It takes a co days for surface water an utaries to swell the Than

Red is the highest league of alerts aimed a authorities.

Amber, the next dow warning to councils to flood precautions.

At the bottom, a means the river catchme is saturated and could fl

'Hungry' man brok into hamburger ba

A HUNGRY Heston man who tried to smash his way into a closed burger bar was presented with a huge bill at Horseferry Road magistrates court.

Prosecutor David Archer told the court that police had seen Anthony Tinney, aged 25, staggering along the Kings Road in Chelsea, at about 11.30pm on December 20th.

Tinney stopped outside the 'American Burger' restaurant and "rattled the door." stated Mr A Police swooped on him they heard the soun breaking glass.

The court heard cleaning staff told police Tinney, of Memorial C had kicked the door in.

"I didn't mean to bre I just pushed the door to if it would open." Ti told magistrates.

He was fined £25 with costs, and ordered to £90.39 in compensation.

Marry sir, it's a secret wedding for Blackadder

BLACKADDER comedy star Rowan Atkinson celebra honeymoon 30,000 ft above the Atlantic yesterday w flew from New York to London after marrying in secret.

His bride was 28-year-old make-up artist Sunetra Stars attending the Variety Club of Great Britain annual business awards yesterday congratulated the couple Rowan, 35, won the award as Top BBC TV Personality.

More awards: Page 3

Gale gang rip off the roof

NG of conmen have made thou-
of pounds by repairing
damaged roofs with cardboard

ce in Southampton were last night
ning three men after a house owner
roof at his home in Southampton
n fixed with the tiles.
told police the workmen charged
ore than £480. A detective said:
iles are useless and get soaked
as soon as it rains."

Another home owner was charged
£900 for a similar job after the gales damaged his roof.

Police said "We are issuing a warning
to people in the aftermath of the storms to
be careful if they are having roof repairs.

"There are a lot of people who are taking advantage of the weather and want to
make a quick profit.

"People should make sure they get a
written estimate and inspect any work
before they part with money."

New storms set to batter Britain

A NEW onslaught of torrential rain –
whipped along by savage winds – is
poised to hit southern Britain today.

A depression gathering over the
Atlantic will bring gales gusting up to
60 mph, forecasters warned last night.

A spokeswoman at the London
Weather Centre did not rule out the
of more storm havoc in Wales
hern England.
oasts will be hardest hit, she said.
the sort of thing we have

seen several times in the last couple
of weeks," she added.

"Anything that's a bit loose and
weak could be damaged."

But the destruction caused by the
January 25 storm, which left 47 people dead, is unlikely to be repeated.

"The wet conditions will be more
of a feature," the expert said.

Weather alerts will go out today to
fire brigades, British Rail and motor-
ing organisations.

DEFIANT MANDELA'S SALUTE TO FREEDOM

ELSON Mandela
merged into the sweet
ir of freedom after 27
ears yesterday ... and
aised his fist in tri-
umph.

He was due to leave his
prison outside Cape Town
at 1 pm our time. But he
kept history waiting for an
extra 75 minutes as he
shared tender private
moments with his family.

Then Mandela, 71, and
his 55-year-old wife
Winnie walked hand in
hand among the waiting

crowd. The man who had
become a symbol of hope
to his people, most of
whom had never even seen
him before, was ready to
play his part in reshaping
the destiny of South Africa.

First he had to face the
chilling reality of his country today. Within hours
police opened fire on a section of the 200,000-strong
crowd waiting to welcome
him in Cape Town.

One youth was reported
killed and up to 200 were
wounded. But many have

given their lives or freedom
in the long struggle to free
Mandela. He paid tribute to
them all when he addressed
the crowd. And he repeated
the plea for a free society
he made at his trial 27 years
ago: "It is an ideal which I
hope to live for and to
achieve. But if needs be, it
is an ideal for which I am
prepared to die."

Mandela also sounded
this ominous warning: "We
have no option but to continue the armed struggle
which we began in 1960."

MIRROR COMMENT

When will she learn?

THERE is a shortage of competent teachers in our schools. And computer
terminals. And text books.

A third of children in primary and secondary
schools are badly educated.

*One lesson in every five in colleges of
higher education is either poor or very poor.*

Standards of reading are low, children near
the bottom of class aren't helped enough, basic
subjects like history and geography often aren't
taught and many teachers have low expectations
of their pupils.

*And in half of all secondary schools
learning suffers because the buildings are
crumbling.*

It was against this background, reported by Her
Majesty's Inspectors of Schools, that Mrs Thatcher
said yesterday that the education system was in far
better shape than it had ever been before.

*What is needed from Mrs Thatcher, apart
from the truth, is less self-satisfaction and
more investment.*

Investment to pay for good teachers (and get
rid of bad ones), to buy books and equipment, to
help pupils who have difficulty learning, to
encourage high expectations and to rebuild the
slum schools.

**Children are the future of Britain. How
can they, or we as a nation, compete
against Europe, America and Japan
unless we spend as much on education
as they do?**

O EXTRA HOURS IN CLASS TO BEAT JAPS

DREN may soon be
to spend an extra two
a day at school to
up with the Japanese.
ore time in front of the
board will improve
rds and give pupils a
grounding in busi-
say education chiefs.
e plan is being put to
s, teachers and public
Tory-run London bor-
of Wandsworth which
over responsibility for
n schools in April.
e council wants to
e the year into four 10-
terms instead of the
term, 38-week school
currently operating in
ns of state schools.
d they hope that sec-
school pupils will
an extra 430 hours a
n class.
nald Naismith, the
gh's director of edu-

by JAMES MEIKLE
Education
Correspondent

cation, said last night: "One
of the reasons the Japanese
are so far ahead of both the
United States and Britain is
that their children work a
staggering two months
more a year in schools.

"We propose our pupils
should start at the normal
time but have the option of
doing an extra third session
from 4pm to 6pm each day
of term.

"They could use this
period to do homework
under supervision, spend
extra time on coursework,
or gain further grounding in
any subject.

"We also want pupils to
take advantage of much
more individualised learning

with computer technology.

"We believe the conven-
tional school day is
organised in such a way
that it's difficult for those
who want to race ahead."
Mr Naismith said teachers
would be paid extra for the
longer hours.

Caution

The Government recent-
ly told some schools to
devote more time to teaching after finding massive
differences in the hours
spent on lessons.

Nigel de Gruchy, of the
National Association of
Schoolmasters–Union of
Women Teachers, said last
night: "In principle we
would not object to after-
hours school, but we would
counsel caution because
teachers are already over-
loaded with work."

Types of News

There are three main types of news, local, national and international. You have already begun to think about the differences between local and national news.

1 Look at the news stories on pages 108–109 and decide what type of news each of these stories is.

Which of these stories did your group find most interesting? Explain your reasons.

Ask your teacher which one she or he found most interesting.

2 Here is how a London radio station covered one of the same stories.

The one o'clock news. This is Julie Benson. The world's most famous political prisoner is about to be set free. Any moment now Nelson Mandela will be released from a small prison near Cape Town in South Africa and driven in a bullet proof car to a huge black rights rally near his home. He's been behind bars for more than quarter of a century for plotting to get rid of white minority rule. From outside the prison, Alison Campbell.

REPORTER: There are upwards of five hundred jubilant people outside the prison, families with picnic baskets, groups of youths dancing under ANC flags, white-haired labourers from surrounding farms and car loads of university students. I asked one group where they'd come from and what their feelings were at this moment.

MAN : We're not satisfied with the strict disciplinary measures which have been taking place here, you know. They're controlling the people and comrades too much because actually Nelson Mandela wouldn't have wanted it like this. He would have wanted everybody to have been in like a festive mood, you know what I mean. So they're always trying to like hassle the people. But the people know that the victory is here, you see, seeing that our leader's been released.

REPORTER: Are you going to have a party tonight?

MAN: We're going to have a party forever.

REPORTER: The police presence is strong but so far there have been no incidents of violence outside the gates of the prison. Alison Campbell, IRN News, Victor Vörster prison, South Africa.

Capital Radio

3 What are the obvious differences between the way the story is handled by the radio and by the newspaper? Make a list of them.

Radio news is sometimes based on newspaper stories. Sometimes it is able to report a story as it is happening. One big difference, however, is that listeners to radio news can hear the words of people directly involved in the news as it happens.

Ordering the News

When you listen to a radio news bulletin, you will notice that there are normally five or six main news stories. The order in which you hear them has been carefully planned, starting with the most important and interesting story. It is the job of the News Editor to decide on that order. She or he will consider whether it is an international, national or local story and how important and interesting it is to the audience. The News Editor will have a clear idea of who the audience for the news programme is.

1 Listen to a news bulletin. Use this chart to help you decide how many main stories there are and what they are about.

Story number	Description of story

Imagine you are a team of people working in the newsroom of a local radio station.

Monday

1 In groups of four look again at the newspaper stories at the beginning of this Unit on pages 108–109 and create a news bulletin based on them.

9.00 It is nine o'clock in the morning. The radio news team are meeting to decide what will be in the one o'clock news.

Decide on your jobs. One of you is going to be the News Editor, one the News Reader and the other two Reporters.

9.05 As part of the news team, you are each involved in deciding which of the stories of the day you are going to cover. First each member of the group chooses his or her own selection of the five stories to be covered.

9.15 The group meets together and discusses which five stories they agree should be presented and the order in which they should appear. The News Editor makes the final decision and gives each story a simple heading, for example, **'Release of Nelson Mandela'.** Use the News Brief Sheet, which also appears as a repromaster in the *Teacher's Resource Book*.

OPERATION Airwaves

OPERATION Airwaves

News Brief

Item 1: Description ....Yes/No
Covered by reporter? ....

Item 2: Description ....Yes/No
Covered by reporter? ....

Item 3: Description ....Yes/No
Covered by reporter? ....

Item 4: Description ....Yes/No
Covered by reporter? ....

Item 5: Description ....Yes/No
Covered by reporter? ....

9.30 Your news station normally sends a reporter to cover two stories. These might be local or national. Each member of the news team has to make his or her suggestions for these two. Again the News Editor has the final decision.

9.45 At this stage the team breaks up. The two Reporters start to prepare their interviews. The News Reader and News Editor work on the script for the news.

12.30 Half an hour before the programme goes out live, the News Editor calls everyone together to have a rehearsal. At this stage you will need a tape-recorder, which will be operated by the News Editor. Run through the script for your news bulletin. While you are doing this, the News Editor should monitor the way it sounds using the station's Airtime Checklist, which also appears in the *Teacher's Resource Book*.

12.45 The team make any necessary changes to take account of the News Editor's comments.

12.50 Have your final rehearsal.

13.00 The one o'clock news is on air. Make a recording of it and write out your group's final version as a script.

OPERATION Airwaves

Notes for the Reporters

1 Decide who you are going to interview. For example, in the Nelson Mandela item, Alison Campbell chose to interview someone waiting outside the prison. The person or people you choose should be able to make the story come alive.

2 Together work out some suitable questions for your two interviews.

3 Make up some suitable answers. You could either do this by interviewing someone else in your class who pretends to be your chosen person. Or you could work these out together, taking it in turns to be reporter and subject.

4 Decide on names for yourselves!

OPERATION Airwaves

Notes for the News Editor and News Reader

1 Prepare a script for the one o'clock news, using the format of the one you have been studying to help you.

2 Leave spaces in the two items for interviews to be added later.

3 The News Reader should practise reading them aloud.

OPERATION
Airwaves

Airtime Checklist

News Reader speaks   too fast / too slowly / at a comfortable speed.*

Reporter 1 speaks   too fast / too slowly / at a comfortable speed.*

Reporter 2 speaks   too fast / too slowly / at a comfortable speed.*

Notes: (Suggest places for pauses, taking breath)

News Reader speaks   all words clearly / most words clearly / speaks very unclearly.*

Reporter 1 speaks   all words clearly / most words clearly / speaks very unclearly.*

Reporter 2 speaks   all words clearly / most words clearly / speaks very unclearly.*

Notes: (Suggest which words should be stressed, which should be spoken particularly carefully)

General Notes: (Add any other helpful comments for members of your news team)

* Ring suitable words.

Tuesday

The director of your radio station is concerned that too much of her station's news output is not relevant enough to young people. As a result, the news team have been asked to prepare a special news bulletin for children of between eleven and thirteen years old.

09.00 You come into work to find this memo on your desk on top of a copy of your local paper.

09.05 Discuss your first reactions to this memo with the other members of your news team. Brainstorm possible subjects for your news bulletin. List them.

09.20 Devise a questionnaire to use in a local school to find out what children of this age are interested in. Remember you will have to keep this simple!

(If possible, some of your group should use this questionnaire with a class from a local school.)

OPERATION
Airwaves

MEMORANDUM

To: All members of the News Team

From: Station Director

Subject: Reaching a younger audience

I am very worried by the recent figures from Audience Research. They show that the number of people between 11 - 13 listening to our station is dropping alarmingly.

This cannot continue.

I am attending a meeting with the Director of Education on Thursday of this week and would like to be able to show her the script for a new kind of programme.

I would like you to research and prepare a lively five minute news bulletin aimed at young people between the ages of 11 - 13.

It must be:

1. About subjects likely to appeal to children of this age range,

2. Written so that they will understand all the words used,

3. Fun!

N.B. You will need to get the views of 11 - 13 year olds at school and listen to other radio programmes for young people.

09.45 Using a local paper, select about ten possible stories. Give each one a heading. For each one make brief notes about why they would be interesting to young children.

10.15 Hold an editorial meeting for all of your news team, using this agenda.

OPERATION
Airwaves

AGENDA

1. Results of questionnaire.

2. List of possible subjects.

3. Possible local stories – each member to present own choice.

4. Agree final list of five subjects / stories.

5. Agree who does what.

First News

I Using some of the techniques which you have developed earlier in this Unit, prepare a five minute radio news bulletin for young people in the eleven to thirteen-year old age bracket.

When you have scripted it, make a tape-recording.

Try it out on your target audience. Ask yourself, can they understand it? Does it hold their interest? Do they enjoy it? Afterwards decide any ways in which your news bulletin might be improved.

Reflection

In this Unit you have been practising how to

● *give a well-organised acccount of an event*
● *ask and respond to questions*
● *use language to convey the news effectively*
● *plan and take part in a group presentation*
● *show that you can use deduction*
● *recognise fact and opinion*
● *produce a questionnaire*

Talk to your friends and your teacher about the things you have been doing in this Unit. Decide how much you have understood and how much progress you have made. Filling in Unit 9 of the Record Sheet on page 118 will also help you think about what you have done in this Unit and the knowledge you are gaining in your English lessons.

Important: Your teacher will give you photocopied versions of these two pages so that you do not need to write in this book.

First of all, with a friend, talk about and decide what the short statements mean. Discuss what you have been practising in English and how much you have understood of what you have done.

Next to each statement there are three targets to aim for. This is what they mean:

I understand this and have practised it.

I have done this with help.

I feel able to do this again.

If you are not sure what a statement means or whether you can do what it says, discuss it with your teacher.

Put a tick under the target that you think best describes what you can do. If you are in doubt, please ask for help.

Name of Student

I can

Unit 7
plan and take part in a presentation (radio pla

contribute to a discussion about a play

read a part in a play

read a radio play

set out a radio play correctly

Unit 8
ask and respond to questions

contribute ideas to a discussion

use language to convey information effectively

show that I understand the difference between fact and opinion

organise information into a list

plan and take part in a group presentation

Unit 9
give a well-organised account of an event

use language to convey the news effectively

show that I can use deduction

recognise fact and opinion

produce a questionnaire

Other comments

Thinking Back

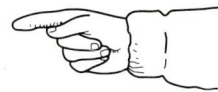

◆ Which is the best piece of work that you have done so far? Why do you think it was particularly successful?

◆ Which of the activities in the last three Units did you enjoy most?

◆ What have you found out about English that you did not know before?

◆ Was there anything you did not understand and would like more help with?

Thinking Forward

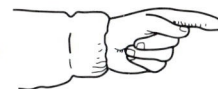

◆ Where do you think you need to improve most? What can you do to help you do so?

◆ What kind of activities can you suggest to your teacher that you could do as extra work?

The Firework Display from *The Fib* by George Layton © George Layton 1978 reprinted by permission of Longman Group UK

Cannonball Simp by John Burningham reprinted by permission of Jonathan Cape Limited

Back to Africa by Louise Bennett reprinted by permission of Sangster's Book Stores Ltd.

Specimen from *Earshot* by David Kitchen reprinted by permission of Heinemann Publishers Ltd.

tombstone and burials register – Oxon Skills Programme 1986, reproduced by permission of the Education Unit, Oxfordshire County Council

programme guides reproduced by permission of the *Radio Times* and the *TV Times*

Orang-Utan by Judith Nicholls, © Judith Nicholls 1990 reprinted by permission of Faber and Faber Ltd. from *Dragonsfire* by Judith Nicholls

interview with Judith Nicholls © Judith Nicholls 1991

The Moth by Stephen Gardam and *The Spider* by Thea Smiley from *Young Words* reprinted by permission of Macmillan, London and Basingstoke

This is Just to Say from *The Collected Poems 1909–1939* by William Carlos Williams, 1987 edition, reprinted by permission of Carcanet Press Limited

Raw Carrots from *Small Poems* by Valerie Worth, copyright © 1972 by Valerie Worth, reprinted by permission of Farrar, Straus and Giroux, Inc.

The Car Trip from *The Hypnotiser* by Michael Rosen, 1988, reprinted by permission of André Deutsch Ltd.

extracts from *Letters to Judy* by Judy Blume, copyright Judy Blume, reprinted by permission of William Heinemann Limited

articles from *The Indy* reproduced by permission of *The Indy* (Young Newspaper Publishing Ltd.)

cover for the Puffin edition of *The Twelfth Day of July* by Joan Lingard (first published Hamish Hamilton Children's Books 1980) copyright © Joan Lingard 1980. Cover photograph by Peter Greenland

articles by school students reprinted by permission of the Middlesex Chronicle (Argus Newspaper Group) – articles produced with the support of the Schools Curriculum Industry Partnership

extracts from holiday brochures reproduced by permission of PGL Young Adventure Ltd., Horizon Holidays, Freetime Leisure Limited

extract from *Moondial* by Helen Cresswell reprinted by permission of Faber and Faber Ltd.

extracts from *Animal Rights* by Miles Barton, reproduced with the kind permission of Franklin Watts, 96 Leonard Street, London EC2A 4RH

baby advertisement reproduced by permission of the National Anti-Vivisection Society Limited

Capital Radio news broadcast transcript reproduced by permission of Independent Radio News

two articles from the Daily Mirror reproduced by permission of Syndication International (1986) Ltd.

Photographs
Bodleian Library 13, 16
British Library 13
Sarah Cavan 112
Clive Barda Photography 28
David Muscroft Productions 29
League Against Cruel Sports 102–105
Tracey Nicholls 57
Chris Ridgers 30, 93
Survival Anglia Photo Library 46
Telegraph Colour Library 26
Tropix Photo Library 24, 88
Bob Watkins 26

Special thanks to Andy Whittle for help and support.

Cannonball Simp pages 18–20
Original paragraph order: P D U R G H E A I J
L N Q S O M T V K X Y W Z B F C

riddle, page 23
The man drove into the desert with a large block of ice in the back of his vehicle. He climbed onto the ice to reach the rope and hang himself. Afterwards the ice melted.

tombstone, page 27
The person buried here is Robert Dawson.